The Flowers Of Spring

Little Whit

Order this book online at www.trafford.com
or email orders@trafford.com

Most Trafford titles are also available at major online book retailers.

Print information available on the last page.

ISBN: 978-1-4907-7789-4 (sc)
ISBN: 978-1-4907-7790-0 (hc)
ISBN: 978-1-4907-7791-7 (e)

Library of Congress Control Number: 2016916950

Trafford rev.   02/14/2017

 www.trafford.com

North America & international
toll-free: 1 888 232 4444 (USA & Canada)
fax: 812 355 4082

Introduction

This story about experiences in the life of Jim Josephson is authentic. The names of the majority of characters and many of the locations are fictitious so their identity may remain in anonymity.

Chapter One

J im met Betsy Lee at an auto mechanics shop on highway ninety eight in Lakeshore Florida. He had gone there to see about the repair of a motor cycle tire, but they didn't work on motorcycles. As Jim approached, a lady walked out the door of the shop. When they greeted each other as she passed by, he thought, "Wow! What a lady." He knew some of the people there, and thought she must be the wife or girlfriend of the owner. He left that day and never returned to that business. They had directed him to Sammy's motorcycle shop, and He had the tire repaired there. He didn't know then the lady was Betsy Lee.

Several years later, He was looking for someone to repair his gold Sun Bug Volkswagen. He had purchased it after he and his first wife divorced. He traded his Plymouth Fury for it because he was driving almost continuously, and it reduced his gas expenses substantially. Roy's Volkswagen repair shop was recommended to him so he decided to go there. He was standing at the counter talking to some of the clerks when this lady walked in. One look at her and her response to him just knocked him off his feet. She went out as quickly as she had come in. He asked one of the clerks: "*Who* was that?" One of them replied: "That's Betsy Lee Harding, Roy Harding's wife, that's who she is." "Who is Roy Harding?" he asked. "He's the owner of this business," She replied. "That's too bad, too bad." he said. She had really caught his attention. Jim went away hoping he would meet her again. He went back several days later to check on his Volkswagen. It was late that day, toward closing time when he arrived. His nephew dropped him off. He knew it would probably be ready. He opened the door and stepped up to the counter. Betsy was seated just inside an office behind the counter. She came out to the counter as she saw him enter. "I came in the other day and left my gold sun bug Volkswagen for Roy to work on. Do you know if it is ready yet?" He asked. "Let me check a moment outside and see." Betsy opened the side door and stepped outside to the work area. Standing there, he thought to himself, "I don't think I have ever seen a person so pleasing to look at. She is so beautiful." He thought about how he had felt when he saw her here the other day. Jim was a bit uneasy there, as he anticipated her reentry. She came back through the door with a big smile and said, "Yes, it's ready. Let me step back into the office and complete the invoice and I'll be right back out." He waited, and after a moment she came back out to the counter with the invoice. "The mechanic will bring it around to the front for you. Look over this invoice and sign it down at the bottom." "Will you take my check?" He asked. "Sure," she said. "Do you need my driver's license?" "No. I won't need that. I know who you are." "You do? How do you know that?" Jim asked. "Well, I remember you from our old place down on ninety eight. I remember you coming in there one day asking about a motorcycle tire." "Oh yeah," He said. "I remember now." Gosh He thought to himself. That was over three years ago. "I saw you there, too." He said. "I just didn't realize that you were you." "I hope I'm me." She laughed. They laughed together, and he could feel a relaxed, shared attraction flow between them. He looked over the invoice. He saw where she had signed it at the top. "Betsy". He signed it at the bottom in bold strokes. He gave her the invoice and proceeded to write the check for the work. As he wrote, he noticed her looking at his signature at the bottom of the invoice. She was fidgeting with her pencil as she looked and had a contemplating expression on her face. He was moved by this. Their eyes met when he handed her the check, and emotion surged through him. He knew she could sense it. She did not resist or turn away. It was a brief but shared moment. "Thank you very much." She said. "Come back if you have other work later on. We appreciate your business." "I will." He said, and looked around to see if his car was there. "It's right over there by that Pontiac Trans Am." She said. "Oh, I see it. Is that your car?" He asked "Yes, it is. That's what I've been driving lately." She said. "I'll see you again one day, as he turned to go out the door." "Ok." she said. He walked over to his gold Volkswagen by the Trans Am. Jim knew she was in a class above him. He was struggling just to keep up with his bills and child support, and He didn't own a home. He had given it to his ex wife when they separated so the children would have a familiar atmosphere after their separation. Jim glanced back inside as he started to open his door. She waved as she saw him look. He waved back, got in his car and left.

Jim went back many times after that to have repair work on his car. As their relationship grew He found excuses to go there, and they talked together often. She drove the Pontiac Trans Am for a while, and then a 280Z. Jim didn't try to see her anywhere else, just at the shop. She was such a kind and considerate person toward him. He didn't know what her personal or social life was like. She was married, though, and he would respect that. She was always very active around the shop, zipping around taking care of business. All of the men around liked her and competed for her attention. Jim believed Roy and one of his colored workers had begun to realize he wasn't coming there just to get his Volkswagen repaired, but they liked getting the business. Jim made a casual relationship with Roy and had begun to like him. He was there one day while they were working on his Volkswagen and walked out into the shop. His car was on the rack. Roy was there. "Well, Roy, are you about to get it?" He asked. "Yeah— he's finishing up. It will be ready in a little while." "You really drive that little car a lot don't you? It has a lot of miles on it since you were here last and that wasn't long ago." "Yeah, I am on the run all of the time. I work three jobs and it keeps me running." Jim said. "I thought you were a teacher." He replied. "I am, but I'm divorced and have children with child support. I work two more jobs to keep up." "What else do you do?" He asked. "Well I work part time at County General Hospital on the weekends and teach Aviation Ground School on Tuesday and Thursday night." "You are a pilot?" He asked. "Yes, I am a civilian pilot. I have an old J3 that I fly a lot. I rent it through a club I have at Lakeshore Airfield. Do you drive race cars?" Jim asked. "I see the race car over there that is being overhauled." "Yes, I build my own cars. I have raced at the Fire Ball Speedway in Lakeshore. I won there one time." He replied. "I race, but it is usually on the highway. There's always somebody that wants to try to get ahead." Jim said. "That's a lot more dangerous than driving the speedway; you never know what they will do next." He chuckled. Jim looked around the shop. He saw a punching bag hanging up over in the corner. Roy was short, stocky and well built. Jim thought maybe he was, or had been, a boxer at one time. He didn't ask him though. He needed to go to the restroom, so he asked Roy if he had a restroom he could use. Roy said, "Yeah, right over there in that corner. You can see the door right there. "Thanks." He said and walked that way. When He opened the door, He got a shock! Pasted on the inside of the door was a full sized, almost completely nude female model with a big smile on her face, and right over the toilet was another one. He moved on out quickly but the experience had started his pulse racing. He looked around for Roy but he was gone. He went back inside where Betsy was and Roy was there with her. It was kind of matter of fact that evening. She just took care of everything and they didn't say much to each other. He could tell she was a little apprehensive with Roy there with them. He went on out to his car where they had parked it over by the road and left for home.

Several weeks had past after that, and one Saturday afternoon as He returned home from work at the hospital on his motorcycle, He saw her car parked at the shop and decided to stop. The parking spaces in front of the shop were empty. He rolled up and parked his bike right in front by the door. He stepped through the door and Betsy was there. No one but the mechanic outside was there. "Hi Betsy, how is everything going?" Jim asked. "Ok." She said. "Everything is a little slow today. What are you doing here? Your car is not here." She asked. "Oh, I just stopped by to say hello. I saw your car parked outside." "Yeah, I'm here by myself this afternoon. Roy went this week to Mexico to see about his family there. He'll be back next week." "You know, Betsy, I thought I might better stop and talk to you a little. It is really great being around you here, but I know it's getting a little stressful for you when I am around. I wouldn't cause you any trouble for anything in the world. I don't want to do anything that would offend you. I respect you too much for that." Jim looked directly into her eyes and said, "I won't come back here again if you will just tell me now not to." She just kept looking straight at him with those beautiful blue eyes of hers, glistening in the evening light, her gaze never wavered, refused to say anything, and let him know in the most moving way, she wanted him to come there. Well, some people talk about cloud nine, Jim was on cloud one hundred! He couldn't believe it was possible; this beautiful lady was really interested in him. He was almost speechless. She said she was always glad to see him, and they appreciated his business. Jim knew even for her, it was more than that. She had made that clear a moment ago. Stumbling for words, he managed to ask her if she would be his friend. She said yes. She would be glad to be his friend. Jim left the shop that evening with mixed emotions. He knew what he wanted more than anything, but he also knew himself and the difficulties that lay ahead.

From then on when they greeted one another, their eyes would always meet with a warm embrace. As time passed by he began to realize he was falling in love with her, whatever that could really mean for him under the circumstances. He could not keep her off his mind. As wrong as it was, he still wanted to be the one in her life so bad. Jim knew he would respect her marriage with Roy though. He knew what had happened to him in his marriage, and wouldn't wish that on anyone.

Jim visited the shop often now, sometimes without any particular reason other than to see and talk with Betsy. They conversed freely with one another, often sharing personal concerns and experiences. Jim came in late one day on his motorcycle, close to closing time. Roy's colored mechanic, Clayton, was there. He was friendly with Jim though and didn't bother Betsy and Jim when they were together. He knew they were friends. He had seen them there together too many times. Jim went through the shop garage and said hello to Clayton and then went on through the side door into the shop. Betsy was in the office working on some papers. You could see into the office through an open entryway. "I just came by for a moment. I didn't know if you were here or not." Jim said. "I'll be out in a moment. I have some work here I need to finish. How have you been?" She asked. "Oh, I've been ok." Jim said. I'll just wait out here until you are finished." "Ok." She said. Jim looked around in the shop at everything. There was a large life size poster of Roy and Betsy standing on a mount next to the counter. Roy was holding a racing trophy, and Betsy was standing close beside him with her arm around his waist. Jim took a seat in one of the chairs, concentrating on the photograph. He thought they really looked great together. The car and background depicted a racing ceremony. He knew Roy must love her and she must love the excitement and attention she gets, he thought. He pondered this with a little remorse. He liked Roy and was a little more than uneasy with his reasons for being there. After a few moments Betsy came out. "Well it's been a while. Where have you been? She asked. "Oh, working mostly. I stay pretty busy. How is everything with you?" He asked. "I've been a little aggravated lately, like just now. I have to do most everything around here now. Roy stays out of the shop a lot, and I have to keep up with all of the paper work and everything." She replied. "I know it must be a difficult job, but you do a good business here. The shop usually stays full." "What good is all of this if you are aggravated all of the time and are not really happy? Roy is so frustrating. You know we lost the house." "No. I didn't know anything about that. I thought you were staying around upstairs to be close to your business at times." "Oh no, I had a wreck back a year or so ago. I rear-ended another car. It really wasn't altogether my fault. We thought we had settled it, but the woman sued. She had whiplash and claimed back injury. We had to sell the house to keep the business and everything. We improvised and made the upstairs an apartment. We've been living up there for a while now. Roy has been so difficult after the lawsuit. It just hasn't been the same. We were happier back at the old place. Sometimes I wish we had never left." "I'm so sorry to hear that, Betsy. It seemed to me that you had everything here." "It has been really difficult. Roy is going his way and I am going mine. It's just been hard for me. Roy gets aggravated at me. He want keep up with everything like he should, which leaves me to do it. I do it right, and sometimes he doesn't like that. You know, taxes and the like. It's not the way I do business. He says not to worry. He'll take care of it and runs off to Mexico. I just don't feel comfortable here anymore." Jim had so many mixed emotions about what he was hearing. He wanted to reach out to her in some way, but he really didn't know what she expected. He knew she was looking for the "good" life, money, affluence, the ability to go when and where she wanted. He also knew she could get anything she wanted. She has long, light sandy brown hair, a gorgeous smile and the most beautiful blue eyes. Her magnetic personality just radiates a warm charisma. She is very considerate and kind, intelligent, ambitious and hard working. No woman had ever touched his heart like she had. "I know what *you* are looking for." Jim said. "You know *I* don't have anything don't you?" "That's too bad, too bad." Betsy said. She knew he had two children from his former marriage because he talked about them a lot. "I have a lot of respect for you, Jim. You just might be what I really need." Jim wanted to say, "Yes! Yes!" — He knew he could give her what she really needed, but he wasn't sure if she thought he could give her what she really wanted. "I really think I could do anything with you by my side" Jim said. "I have so many friends, Roy is aware of that. He knows a lot of men are interested in me. He isn't concerned too much about things like that though. He cares for me I know, and I worry sometime about what he might do. It's not just because of me though, Jim. It's everything that goes with this business and our life together." Jim looked outside and saw Clayton, coming toward the door. "Here comes Clayton." Jim said. "I'll talk with you again sometime soon. I'll have to be going on now. I have to meet with my father at home and he is expecting me." Clayton came on in. "I've got ever thing shut down, Miss Betsy. The 75 green Volkswagen is finished. He can pick it up tomorrow. I'm going on to the house. I will see you in the morning, Miss Betsy." He turned to Jim. "How are you doing, Mr. Josephson? It's sure good to see you here." "Thanks, Clayton, take care and be careful out there." Jim said. "I certainly

will, Mr. Josephson, and you take *real good* care yourself too." He
replied. Jim turned to Betsy as he left. "Well, I need to be going.
I have to get this old motorcycle back to the house. I know Dad
will be waiting for me. I'll see you again next week sometime
probably. You take care and be careful." Jim said. "That Clayton!
He's something else." She said. "Bye, Jim. I'll see you next week."
Jim went out the door to his red motorcycle parked outside. He
backed it up, fired it off and zipped out of the parking lot.

Jim began to do a little searching after that. He inquired
around without letting anyone know what he was really trying
to find out. He went to bars and talked with the locals to find
out more about Roy. He knew He needed to know more about
Betsy and her family. Several times he talked to her about her home
town, Taylorville, Alabama. He talked to her about church and
asked if she attended church anywhere, and she said she did at one
time when she was in Taylorville. Later he went to Taylorville and
drove around looking for the place she may have lived. He went
down a road by a field and had this strange feeling that she had
been there. He stopped his car and got out. A house was across
the street from the field so he walked over there. He looked on the
mailbox and there was her maiden name. Jim thought to himself,
"My goodness she probably *ha*s been here. Maybe she lived here
once." Jim knocked on the door, but no one answered. Later on
back in Lakeshore, He mentioned this place to Betsy Lee and asked
her who might have lived there. Laughingly she said; "Probably one
of your girl friends." Well, this was just what Jim wanted to hear
and he was elated about what had happened and what she had said.

Jim began to talk to Roy more also and got to know him
quite well. He learned he is of Mexican descent from Pine Hill,
Alabama, so *he* said, a place near Taylorville, where Betsy Lee grew
up. Jim had learned not to take everything Roy said too seriously.
He knew already that his family lived in Mexico. He is a very
interesting character and has a pleasing appearance. He has sky
blue eyes and is stocky built with long wavy hair and a muscular
upper body, probably from lifting weights and using the punching
bag. Jim could see why a woman would be attracted to him. Jim

came there one day and they began talking together in the office in the shop. They talked about a lot of different things. It was as if he was trying to find out more about this "teacher" that had been hanging around his shop so much lately. They talked a lot about airplanes, engines and cars. Roy had actually built their house himself, the one they had to sell. They talked some about carpentry and building. Roy was amazed that Jim knew so much about so many different things. He didn't expect that from a school teacher. He didn't think school teachers knew very much about the "real" life of the street. He invited Jim upstairs to their apartment. Betsy Lee was there. They had drinks and began to socialize. He had a pool table and invited Jim to play. He didn't know Jim could play with the best of the local pool sharks. He agreed to play, and with Betsy Lee watching; He beat her husband handily. The school teacher had surprised him again. Jim wasn't really proud of that though in retrospect. He liked Roy and really felt guilty about how he felt about his wife although he knew she had lost her deepest feelings for him. He seemed to know of Jim's interest but didn't seem worried much about it. It was as though he had some hidden control over her. She seemed submissive around him and appeared sometimes to be afraid of him.

Jim never tired to meet Betsy Lee anywhere because he personally felt approaching another man's wife was wrong even though a lot of what was happening wasn't really right. He knew she went to parties frequently with her friends, often without Roy. Jim wasn't privy to those relationships she had and just vaguely knew about them. Often Roy would take trips to Mexico. He had relatives there. Jim had a suspicion he was running drugs from Mexico but he didn't know for sure. He had learned from the grapevine some local officials thought he was. Several times Betsy Lee also went to Mexico. Jim talked briefly to her once by innuendo, feeling her out about this activity, hinting that he might try it for her, since he wasn't a wealthy person. Jim really had no intention of doing this though. Her comment was, "It only takes once." Jim was taken back a little by this. He never attempted to learn any more about it. He spoke to her again later on about how she inspired him. How he thought he could accomplish most anything for her because he would be motivated to try to reach his highest potential. He knew she didn't realize his real potential with the right kind of woman encouraging him. She had commented once that he might be just what she needed. Jim knew then what she was probably questioning inside; He was really what she wanted and needed, but she wasn't sure he could give her the lifestyle she really wanted. At times, Jim felt Roy might be threatening her because of her obvious interest in him. He wondered if Roy had told Betsy he would "take care" of him if she made any moves toward him, because he had begun to see the shadier side of Roy's life. He also knew that Betsy was caught up in the shadier part of his life.

Once one Friday afternoon about two o'clock, when Roy was away on one of his "trips", Jim carried his Volkswagen to her shop to have a tune up and plug change. Clayton was working on his car. Jim and Betsy Lee were talking and having coffee. They had been together for some time. Jim stepped outside to see how things were going. Betsy Lee came outside with him. While Clayton was under the car working, Jim looked across the car to Betsy Lee on the other side. They didn't say anything to each other. Their eyes met with an emotional embrace. Jim could feel his heart pounding and both of them began to be filled with deep feeling and desire. This was interrupted when Clayton stood up from the car and said he had broken something; stripped a plug thread he thought, and could not fix the car until the next day. Jim turned to Clayton and said: "Are you sure you can't fix this today Clayton? I have to pick up my children in River Springs this evening and need the car." "No sir Mr. Josephson. That plug just went and stripped out. I don't have the tool to fix it here now. I'm sorry sir Mr. Josephson." Betsy walked up to them. "Don't worry Jim. I'll take you to get your children." "Gosh Betsy, they live in River Springs that's twenty miles or more away." Jim said. "It's closing time. I'll close the shop and take you there to get them. We have a car for that." Jim thought about all it would involve and what might be about to happen. "You would have to drive all the way over to River Springs and then back." He said. "That's over forty miles." "Really, I don't mind Jim." "Well—ok—you can take me there to get them." Jim said hesitantly. "Ok, Miss Betsy", Clayton said. "I'll shut down the garage and go on to the house. I can get what we need to fix it Monday Probably." Jim followed Betsy into the shop. She closed down everything, locked up, and they went outside. After they got into the Volkswagen she used for the service car, Jim thought again about what might be about to happen. He asked her to just take him home. He would find a way to go get them. This was the first time he had been alone with Betsy Lee away from the shop and he could feel the powerful attraction they had for one another. As they rode along they hardly spoke except for the directions he was giving her. She seemed to be contemplating something important very deeply. When they stopped in front of his house, they both turned and looked at each other. Jim never wanted to embrace and kiss anyone more in his life and he could tell she wanted him to. Jim hesitated for a moment and almost reached out to embrace her but stopped short. He thanked her, said goodbye, opened the door and left.

Jim tried hard to explain to himself why he could not bring himself to kiss her. He didn't know if it was his relationship with Roy, knowing inside it was wrong, or just his own fear of rejection, which he really knew was next to impossible. And yet, as strange as it seems, it was probably because he really loved her. He loved her with the deepest love. Not just a physical need which was powerful and present, but with the deepest reaches of his heart. He knew she could sense he had fallen in love with her. He didn't want his relationship to be based on anything that was wrong.

After this, Jim became bolder and Roy became more suspicious of him. Jim thought Clayton must have told him they had left the shop together. Roy was very nervous around him and he could sense his irritation. Late one night shortly after this occurred; Jim got a phone call at home. It was Roy. He said he had a specially built racing Volkswagen engine that would last "forever" in his car and he wanted him to come over there that night and look at it. Jim had a feeling that something was up. Jim had noticed an emotional inflection in his voice that gave away his anxiety. "Well, Jim thought quickly, I've got myself into this situation and I am not going to cower. I will just go and face the music." He really felt Roy was going to confront him and maybe try to whip his butt, which he was afraid he just might be able to do since he may have been a boxer. Jim put on his corduroy suit, put his thirty–eight derringer in his right coat pocket and drove over to Roy's shop on highway ninety eight. He and Clayton were there and the shop was dark. No one else was there. Jim thought: "Uh oh, I'm in trouble now." They went over together to open the workshop door. When Jim reached up to help them push up the door, Clayton saw the derringer in his suit pocket. They went inside. Jim kept his hand in his right coat pocket on the cocked derringer. He noticed Clayton was watching carefully. Roy appeared a little nervous. Jim watched his position all of the time so as not to lose any advantage by being between the two of them. Roy explained all of the parts, the price he was asking and everything. It was really a good deal but Jim wasn't there to make a deal and he wasn't sure Roy was either. He refused his offer and they went back outside. Jim left in his Volkswagen to go back home. He breathed a sigh of relief that neither one of them had died that night. It could have very easily been either one of them. He was sure Roy had realized, with Clayton's help, what a dangerous position he had been in. When Jim got home, he un-cocked his derringer and opened the breech to take out the cartridges and it was empty! His heart skipped a beat.

Jim thought long and hard after that about what was unfolding. He knew Roy was probably on to everything now. Roy knew Jim was aware of his questionable activities. Jim thought sometimes Roy might believe he was an undercover agent. He wondered if Roy might be trying to convince Betsy that he was an agent. That made him question a little in his mind why Betsy was so friendly toward him, but he just couldn't believe that was her intention. He knew that things were getting complicated. His principal at the school where he taught, Mr. Mixon, had been asking some strange questions. One day he was complimenting him for having so much rapport with students. He was really impressed, he said. Even the most incorrigible students seemed, he said, to have the utmost respect for him. "You can paddle a student Jim, and I never hear a word about it from the community." Mr. Bush, the math teacher, can paddle one and half the community is here the next day complaining." The conversation went on about his activity around the area. Locals had seen him often in various places in the deep woods around the area. Jim related to the principal what he already knew, because he knew all of Jim's family. He was a hunter, and he frequented the forest area around the school a lot because he loved the country and woodlands. He mentioned that his dad and uncle had hunted quail and turkeys for years in these woods, a fact many locals already knew. He really began to wonder though when his principal commented: "Some people in the community want to know how a teacher can afford an airplane." He hadn't questioned him specifically, but Jim began to realize where he was coming from. Jim explained how he had a club at the field and the club was actually paying for the plane. The J3 was an airplane that almost every pilot wanted to fly, but couldn't. It was an antique and owners would not let just anyone fly them. He was doing a great business with the plane and was making money. His discussion seemed to relieve any apprehension his principal might have had. He was a great friend and trusted Jim completely. Only one thing prevented them from being an unbeatable team together. Mr. Mixon, was a very conservative Republican and Jim was a moderate Democrat. Jim realized now what was happening. Some officials in the county were probably beginning to believe that he was involved in the drug business because of his association with Roy, his aircraft ownership, and his other activities. He had learned from his own covert inquires that Roy was being investigated undercover for trafficking in drugs. Jim was never questioned outright but he knew he was right one day when officers showed up at his school with drug dogs. They made a point to specifically check his truck. Jim heard through the grapevine that he was just too smart for them. They couldn't catch him. "Boy!" Jim thought to himself. "I'm in the middle of something here and I had better watch my step. It had become difficult and dangerous for Jim when his questionable activity had unjustly compromised his reputation, and heartfelt desire had compromised his better judgment.

Jim really didn't know for sure where Betsy Lee stood in all of this, but he was sure Roy had control and influence over her, most likely in a threatening manner, because she was privy to everything he had done and was doing. Jim wondered what her personal life might be like. After all, she had said she was going her way and Roy was going his. At the time, Jim had thought she was opening the door for him. Rationally Jim knew his interest in her was not the best thing. Their inherited physical rhythms and attractions coupled with deep spiritual feeling and emotion were what had moved his heart though. He knew this just sometimes happen to innocent people and their lives are forever changed. Jim's family's expectation of him, his own expectations of himself, and his own personal values were being challenged. Reluctantly, for her sake and his, he knew he would need to withdraw for a while.

Chapter Two

After Jim's divorce from his first wife, he had gone to live with his elderly mother and father. It was not an advantage for him, but they needed him there and Jim wanted to spend some time with them. He knew the good times with them were soon coming to a close. He had a great childhood there. His dad was a carpenter, a short but powerfully built man with a very mature and humble personality. He was very intelligent and could do most anything well. His schooling had ended after the eighth grade when he began to work to help support their large family. The family was located in the deep forest and the men worked in the timber and naval stores business. Times were hard in 1930 when Jim's dad and his mother married. They lived with his dad's family there on Yellow River for a brief period before moving to town to live with Jim's mother's family.

Jim's dad struggled to make a living at first. It was the time of the deep depression, so they didn't have many things, but they had the love of two very large families. His dad had seven brothers and four sisters. They all had families and cared for each other as close families do. Jim's mother was a hard working Christian woman everyone loved. She had two brothers and four sisters. She was a gracious and caring lady. She loved her husband deeply and without question. One of Jim's dad's brothers, Oliver, and his wife, Sarah, lived next door. Sarah was also his mother's sister. They were very close to his Uncle Oliver and Aunt Sarah because they had no children. Jim and his sister Mary became their children also. They lived, together there as one family. Jim, his dad, and his uncle next door did everything together as he grew up. They worked together, hunted together and fished together. They deer hunted with their other brothers on Yellow River where their old home had been. When the deer season closed, they quail hunted with dogs until that season closed, usually at the end of February. In the last of March and the first of April, they turkey hunted for turkey gobblers. They hunted quail and turkeys most often in the forest north of Lakeshore around the school where Jim eventually came to teach. They fished on Parmer Lake and Yellow river for bass and brim. The best times Jim had with his dad were up Boiling Creek, off Yellow River, bait casting for bass.

When Jim was a young boy, most of the recreation and fun he had was with his Dad and Uncle Oliver. Most of his young life was spent with them working, helping with the needs of his Mother and Dad's families, and hunting and fishing. Jim had friends and companions in the neighborhood that were his age. Cousins from his mother's side of the family, and others lived close by. They engaged in the usual activities young boys find interesting; hunting, fishing, building things and playing games. But the activities with his father and his father's family were special. Hunting and fishing with them and their family were exclusive. It was a family affair. Jim's young friends and companions did not share the activities he had with his dad and uncle and their friends. In this respect, Jim was a member of a man's world beginning at a very young age. They were such great men. They reflected in real life the values Jim was being taught as a Christian, but they were not members of the church. Jim never regretted this exclusiveness one bit and the association accelerated his maturity. He became a serious and responsible person at a very young age. He had no room for frivolous things. Jim's men friends had such maturity and character. They didn't engage in frivolous activities of any kind. Their hunting and fishing activities were more like work. It was like working to get food for the family as they had to do back in their days at home on Yellow River. One could say it this way, work was a pleasure to them. They loved to engage in meaningful things that satisfied some need for their family.

Jim's mother and her sister were responsible for his religious education. They were devout Presbyterians and saw to it that he engaged in the activities of the church at an early age. The relationship he had with his father and father's family gave him a more purposeful outlook on life. He took everything about Christianity seriously, from the very beginning. He had an inquisitive mind, however. He weighed and contemplated things. He thought for himself. He had the mind of an objective realist and the heart of a spiritual mystic.

He engaged in a lot of deer and quail hunting with his father's family. His dad and uncle were deer hunters first, but after the deer season they hunted for quail every chance they got. His Dad got hooked on quail hunting after his Uncle Oliver introduced him to the sport in an area above Munson Florida in the 1930s. They would talk about walking the branches and hills of the area and finding coveys of quail on just about every ridge and holler.

Jim hunted with his friends in the area around his home with air rifles and slingshots when growing up. He was given a shotgun for Christmas when he was in the seventh grade in school. That's when he started hunting with his Dad and Uncle. Jim managed to take four bucks hunting with the party of brothers. One small buck was taken with an archery shot from a short Turkish re-curve bow after being stalked on the ground to within thirty yards. He loved to hunt quail with his Dad and Uncle. There was always action. If they weren't shooting at quail, they were walking and watching dogs work in beautiful country, primarily Blackwater State Forest. His Uncle Oliver had some great bird dogs back then. He began hunting behind his dog Sport, a liver and white Pointer. After Sport came Mack, a black and white setter. Mack was paired later with a liver and white pointer named Blaze. What great dogs they were. Jim loved the dogs. They were his friends and he had as much command over them as his Uncle and Dad.

What great men he was blessed to be around. For starters they didn't smoke, drink, curse, or gossip. Well, his uncle Oliver would use profane language when he got angry at something important. They never argued with one another. They were tough as whet leather, honest and truthful as the day is long, and all of this was very important to them. Their father had instilled in them these values and it made being with them some of the most important times in Jim's life. They would hit the bird hunting country at daybreak and walk until sundown with just a short break for lunch. They never complained about anything and they didn't like it if you did, so Jim didn't. He made it his business to stay with them every step and you can know with every step he had the greatest respect and love for them that a person could have. The word "love" was not used often by the men of his father's family back then. They didn't openly express feelings like that easily. Their values instilled in Jim a strong desire to be honest, truthful, hard working and upright in everything he did. His Christian teaching and experience magnified this desire even though his Dad and Uncle were not church members. Jim's Mother reflected these very same values in her role as a wife and homemaker. Jim was a blessed person and it didn't take long for him to realize that. A great relationship between people like a father and son is a two way thing. Each one must be responsive toward the other. Jim could see years later from comments his mother made that he was as much responsible for the relationship they developed as they were because he had responded to their example and teaching. They saw that in him and it amplified their love and influence.

Money was hard to come by back then, as the saying goes. Jim would pick up drink bottles and collect a deposit for them from the local merchants. He picked up pecans in season from trees along roadways and in vacant lots and sold them to local merchants. He worked with his Dad starting when he was old enough to be able to. In the beginning, he helped with whatever his dad was doing, whether it was just fixing something at home or working for someone else. His dad would contract local carpentry jobs. Sometimes he contracted the trim with construction companies and Jim would work with him to complete the jobs. Jim never bartered for wages. He never asked his dad to pay him anything. Jim never expected him to. They were working for the family. If it was a job where money was received for the work they did, his dad always gave him a share. Jim never asked for any and he never questioned what his dad gave him. Jim went with his Uncle through the country in north Florida and south Alabama buying chickens and pecans sometimes. Jim enjoyed this immensely. His uncle would pay him for that.

Once when Jim was about thirteen years old, He had been paid twenty dollars for work he had done and was going to Wilson's Hardware to buy some shotgun shells with it. The hardware was located where the old James Williams Hardware had been, on River Road right past the end of Thames Street. Jim rode his bicycle down to the hardware store. He went inside and was asked by the clerk, who was Mr. Wilson, what he was looking for. Jim said he wanted two boxes of twelve gauge, size eight shotgun shells. They were inside a glass counter right by the cash register. Mr. Wilson got the shells, put them in a bag and placed them on the counter. He said they would be seven dollars and seventy two cents. Jim handed him his twenty dollar bill for payment, a considerable amount of money for him back then. Mr. Wilson opened the cash register, put the bill in the till and gave Jim his change. Jim looked at the change and it was two dollars and twenty eight cents. He looked up at Mr. Wilson and said, "Mr. Wilson, I gave you a twenty dollar bill! Jim didn't know what to expect at the moment. He didn't know how Mr. Wilson would react, if he would believe him. He quickly stated, "Oh yes! I believe you did give me a twenty dollar bill." He opened the cash register, took a bill from the till and handed it to Jim over the counter. Jim had removed the shells from the counter and he turned to leave. He looked down at what he had. He had the shotgun shells, two dollars and twenty eight cents change and a twenty dollar bill in his hand. Jim paused for a moment, thinking about what he had. He turned around to Mr. Wilson who was still standing behind the counter and said, "Mr. Wilson, I know something about you. You are an honest man." "How do you know that?" He asked. "Because you reached into the ten dollar till to give me the right change and gave me my twenty dollar bill back. You had put it there thinking it was a ten." Jim put the shells, the two dollars and twenty eight cents and the twenty dollar bill back on the counter. Mr. Wilson looked at Jim and said, "I know something about you. You are and honest man too." He took the twenty and gave him back a ten. Jim went away from there with the greatest feeling. He had experienced an opportunity, in the face of strong temptation, to be as honest and fair as his father was. That was the kind of influence his Dad and Uncle had on him. Jim wanted to honor their reputation so much. And besides, Mr. Wilson had called him a man. Jim wasn't always like that, but they had moved him there, not by their preaching, but by their example and by their love. Of course, Jim was also influenced by the Biblical Scriptures that he read over and over even as a young child, especially Isaiah and the Psalms. He was always so proud of his Dad. He was proud he was a carpenter like Jesus was a carpenter. When someone would ask what his father did and Jim told them he was a carpenter, those thoughts would come to mind because he knew his Dad was very much like the way Jesus had taught us to be.

Jim and his dad always did business with Mr. Wilson when they could. They always knew he would be fair and treat them right.

Jim had a great life there at home. Mary, his sister, was six years older than Jim. She shared all of this good fortune and later became a nurse. She enrolled at Saint Margaret's School of Nursing in Montgomery, Alabama after she graduated from high school. They would take her back to nursing school often, after a vacation or break. One spring they went in his dad's old nineteen forty seven Ford. Jim was only about twelve years old at the time. Grandmother Carter (his mother's mother) lived with them there at her old home place in Lakeshore, and she went with them. Jim, his mother and dad, Uncle Oliver and Aunt Sarah, Granny Carter, and Mary, his sister, all crammed into the old car, and departed for the trip. They traveled to State Highway Eighty Seven and then to U.S. Highway Thirty One at Brewton Alabama and on up through Castleberry, Evergreen, McKenzie, Georgana, Greenville and Fort Deposit to Montgomery, Alabama.

Everyone would be captivated with the scenery as they traveled the old roads and all of them would enjoy each other's excitement and fascination at what they saw. They were a great family together. The love they had for one another was unique and very special.

They would never tire of each other's stories and comments. Everyone was loved and respected by everyone else. There was never any tension or argument of any serious nature between any of them. Aunt Sarah would get a little nervous at times but things would always work out because of their caring.

Granny Carter was a lover of flowers and the Alabama highways were just beautiful with all kinds of wild flowers. The air was filled with the fragrance and joy of spring, and their hearts were filled with the joy, love and companionship of a very close family.

Happiness would turn to sadness however, as they left Jim's sister at the School and started to return home. Of course, his mother and Aunt Sarah would cry. They couldn't help it, they loved her so much. You could even see a glimmer in the eyes of the two men that Jim loved so much. Jim would feel heartbroken, and would think to himself, "I hope I never have to go off to a place like that!" The trip back always had a different mood. It was because Jim's sister was missing.

Jim often reflected on those trips as the years passed. He knew he and his sister were very blessed to have been part of this loving family. And he knew why each spring when the flowers begin to bloom and the air was filled with their fragrance, that deep down his heart was filled with joy and peace, no matter how difficult the events of life had become. He knew it was because of the great memories and love he was given by this family. So much so that he always possessed a hope for the less fortunate in the world, that they too, somehow could experience the joy, love, peace and happiness that they did. Jim always had a desire and a vision to somehow give back to others this holy gift that was given to him.

Jim was sexually precocious as a child, but the discipline and love he had at home enabled him to restrain and discipline himself. He had a powerful drive at an early age but didn't let it be outwardly known as best he could. The girls always fascinated him. Even in the first and second grades he could remember kissing the girls in the old cloak room at school. He had many childhood infatuations of the child kind. Of course, none of his family knew anything about any of this. It was too embarrassing for him. He was too bashful then. The girls always seemed to have an attraction for him as he did for them. He was about twelve years of age when his sister enrolled in nursing school in Montgomery, Alabama. She would bring some of her friends to visit with their family on occasions. One of her friends, Betty Jenison, was joking and teasing at Jim one day. Well, she began teasing him about boy-girl relationships. She could sense his interest in her. One of her comments was: "You wouldn't know what to do with it." She didn't realize that even at that age, Jim was as mature as any man would be and more so than most. Jim was also capable of self discipline more so than most. He valued good and proper relationships with others because they were valued by the people he loved. Another one of Mary's really close friends and her family came to visit their humble home once. Jim could sense that they were much more affluent than his family. They were, however, the most kind and gracious people toward them. Their daughter, Barbara Whitcomb, was a friend of Mary's at the nursing school. She was the pretty, cute type and was very friendly with Jim. No one knew it, but Jim had become amorously attracted to her. Their families went to the state fair in Lakeshore and she rode the scary rides with Jim when no one else would, and to him it was great. She was just like a girl friend to Jim even though she was much older. Jim always remembered her as a friend and companion. Jim had several girl friends through middle school and on in to high school. He didn't have the social graces or capability to actively "court" any of these girls except at school. His first real "love" affair (it was just an affair of the heart) happened when he was a junior in high school. He fell in "love" with one of his classmates. She came from a fairly affluent family and was already dating a much older boy who had everything he needed to take her out and "court" her. Embarrassingly, all Jim had was the time at school. He didn't have a car, and he didn't have a driver's license. This didn't stop him from attracting her attention, and by the middle of his senior year, he had captured a part of her heart. She surely had captured all of his. It was too late however; she had become pregnant by the other suitor and had to marry him before she finished high school. Jim thought the pregnancy had happened before they began to really like each other later on. No one but she and Jim knew anything about their attraction except maybe their teachers. Jim's heart was broken, but he took it in stride. He was heartsick over her for a long time after that.

Jim's dad never once attempted to teach him how to drive or help him obtain a driver's license during his high school years. His Uncle Oliver did do some of this, but his help was limited because he didn't want to infringe on his dad's role as a father. Jim's dad never took time to teach or encourage him in athletics or other sports activities. He was not a socializer other than with his family. Of course he attended the traditions of society that involved friends and family. They went to marriages, funerals, reunions and gatherings that involved the family, but he did not engage in Church or other social activities. Jim never went to a football or baseball game with him. Never went to a Church social or other social activity of that nature with him. Jim's dad did go to his Father and Son FFA Banquet when he was a senior in High School. Jim taught himself how to do the things his dad was skilled in doing because he loved him so much. He taught himself the carpentry skills his dad possessed through passive observation as he acted as a helper when he was a young boy. His dad never aggressively or purposefully taught him anything like that, except by observation and example. Of course he would correct him when he saw him doing something incorrectly or offer suggestions when he faced some difficulty. Jim learned primarily by observing him. Jim's dad knew his son was acquiring the skills he had because he would give him responsibilities that required the skills he possessed. Jim knew his dad was an expert boat handler. He could scull a river boat with power and precision backward or forward, right hand or left. Jim had watched him while fishing many times, so he taught himself in an old waterlogged boat in a bayou off the river behind his home. He became the best boat handler in his family, the best quail shot with a shotgun. Eventually Jim was his dad's equal with carpentry skills. Jim and his dad went fishing once on

Parmer Lake off Yellow River shortly after Jim had taught himself to scull a boat. Jim had fished for some time, bait casting, when his dad asked him to come back to the stern of the boat and see if he could keep the boat steady for his dad to fish. Jim started sculling the boat around like a professional. His dad said to him, "When did you learn to scull a boat like that!?" Jim swelled with pride as he related to him how he had done this on his own over in the bayou. "How did you convince your mother to let you do this?" He asked. "She never knew anything about it." Jim said. Their relationship grew around this shared ability. They were great bait casters for bass because they could both fish and handle the boat to perfection. Jim learned to pitch a baseball, but he taught himself. His dad was an accomplished pitcher in the County League way back but never attempted to teach Jim anything about it, and he never asked. Partly because of his dad's passiveness and lack of motivation toward him in that regard, Jim never found the opportunity to play in organized sports though he excelled in most physical endeavors. Jim had a chance to engage football in the tenth grade but a fractured clavicle put an end to that opportunity. Most of their activities together involved working, hunting and fishing, and Jim thoroughly enjoyed every minute of it. He learned to drive the hard way with Uncle Oliver's help driving his work truck, but never obtained a license until after high school. Jim loved his dad so much he never thought about what was happening until much later in life. His mother related to him what had happened. His dad was attempting to discipline him with corporal punishment when he was too young to remember, and his Grandmother Carter intervened aggressively. Jim's mother and dad lived with her there at her homestead. Jim's mother told him his dad never had anything more to do with his discipline or teaching after that. Regretfully she complimented, "It's a wonder, Jim—your father never would have anything to do with your development when you were growing up, but you learned to love him so deeply." Jim never knew the difference then. He just thought that was the way he was. Jim knew later in life his dad appreciated very much how he felt about him and all of the things he had learned to do, basically on his own, emulating him. They became the greatest of friends. His dad realized what Jim could do and was very proud of him. One of the proudest moments of Jim's life was when he showed his dad his score on the State of Florida Master Teacher Test in Science under Governor Bob Graham's Master Teacher Program. Jim had scored in the ninety–eighth percentile and had earned the Master Teacher designation. He related it was competition between college graduates in science and he had bettered ninety eight percent of them. His dad swelled with pride. Jim could see it, and he could not have felt better had he been talking to the President of the United States. No one else needed to know at the time and very few did. His dad knew, and that was all that mattered to Jim. His dad's formal education had ended with the eighth grade, but Jim felt he was much smarter than he was. He loved him so much. His dad had such integrity and character. He was very humble yet strong, and everyone loved him.

Jim was very active in his Mother's family church (The Lakeshore Presbyterian Church) during his high school years. Whiting Field Naval Aviation Training Station was nearby and some of the Naval Officers had active leadership roles in the Church. Jim knew two of them well. They both had daughters who were about Jim's age. One was very pretty and could sing really well. Jim eventually dated her some when he was in college even though he was older. Her family knew Jim would treat her as a Christian should. They were eventually transferred to Hawaii. Jim lost more than a little sleep over her. As a matter of fact, he withdrew a hard fought registration as a junior at the University of Florida partly because of her. The other one, though, was a real go getter. She was not as pretty as the other girl but came on strong. It was very hard for Jim to resist her advances although he was not especially attracted to her. One of the elders of the church had a beautiful daughter, April. He and his wife were very close friends with Jim's mother and Aunt Sarah. They tried very hard to bring the two of them together, both families. They literally grew up together in the church. They went to the church socials and football games together but not as "dates". Jim really didn't have the means (he thought) to actively court her during this time. Her father was a banker, and they were in a different social class. The pastor and others were encouraging Jim to become a minister, and Jim knew April was impressed with that. Jim was given the opportunity to lead. He could speak well and was well liked by the church members. He loved the bible but viewed it more as an inspired work of the writers, and in his mind, questioned its complete infallibility. Deep down he knew, eventually, he would have to question some of their deeply held traditions. Jim knew he would get all of the support he needed if he chose the ministry. He knew April really liked him. He didn't know how much because he wouldn't let her get too close to him. Jim had feelings for her and thought about the possibilities, but the other girl in school was stealing his heart at the time and he let it pass.

His sister, Mary, married one of her high school friends when he returned from the Army after serving a tour in Korea during the Korean Conflict. Mary was a nurse for a local physician for a while and later for the Lakeshore Memorial Hospital. She had four great sons from this marriage, but it encountered difficulty. They divorced, only to be remarried later in life. During the time they were separated by divorce, Mary and the boys lived next door to the old home where Jim and their Mother and Father lived. Jim spent a lot of time mentoring the three older boys during this time. He loved them like they were his own sons. He encouraged his dad and Uncle to include them in all of the hunting activities that they undertook. Jim knew this activity would shape their lives for "good" because of the relationship they would have with him, his Dad, and Uncle Oliver. Jim's dad and Uncle Oliver were to them as they had been to him as a young boy, a tremendous influence for good in their lives.

After high school Jim decided to enter the military. Jim's Dad and Uncle Oliver offered to help him attend Lakeshore Junior College if he would choose college over the military. He decided to attend college and enrolled at Lakeshore Junior College. April had been dating John Carter, a church friend of Jim's, who was also from an affluent family in town. He was older than April and was also enrolled at the college. One day when Jim and his friend John were having cokes in the Student Union, John spoke to him about April. He said he was going to marry her and asked Jim if it was all right with him. Jim said sure, it was all right with him, but he wondered about this for a long time. Jim knew John must have known April was interested in him, but he would never fully respond. Jim really thought she may have been in love with him. John and April married, but before April was twenty-five years old, she died of cancer. Jim was grieved over this for many years. For some crazy reason, he really felt had he married her, April wouldn't have died. He knew this made no scientific sense whatsoever, but nevertheless, this feeling was strong within him. Years later, her mother in a conversation concerning April would say to him: "You just wouldn't give anyone a chance". Jim knew what she was talking about, and he was saddened. Jim loved them dearly, and he knew she was right. Jim had given up the girl and the ministry.

Jim's childhood had also given him the ability to love deeply and sincerely. He was blessed with a profusion of emotion and had an interest in almost everything. His hard working and sporting life with his dad had made him physically fit. Jim was thin and moderately tall, hard as nails, and deceptively strong. He could compete with almost anyone in physical activities. Of course he knew there were people who could out do him, but he could handle himself very well. Jim had strong self-esteem embellished with lots of ego and pride. After he finished college and before he met his first wife, he had become a ballroom dancer, trained in the art by Arthur Murray Studios in Lakeshore. He had learned to move with poise and confidence, and he did. He loved all of the arts, although he majored in science (Medical Technology and Science Education). Jim could draw well and loved music. He taught himself to play guitar. He sang bass in the Church choir.

He met his first wife, Edith, at Author Murray Studios. She was divorced and had one small boy, Sandy Whitmire. She was a beautiful woman and had several suitors. Jim competed for her hand for about a year and finally she accepted his marriage proposal. They were married in the Lakeshore Presbyterian

Church of his youth. They were a great couple together. They were sociable, active and everyone liked them. Jim was a salaried Medical Technologist at Lakeview Hospital in Lakeshore at the time. After Junior College he had received his four year degree in Medical Technology from a college in Alabama and trained, ironically, in the same hospital he had traveled to as a boy, where his sister had trained as a nurse. He was contemplating attending Medical School. He was making arrangements to take the medical entrance examination. Marrying Edith stopped that short, however. Edith soon delivered Jim's first child, Aaron. All of their families were excited. They didn't have much, though and it bothered Edith. Soon after that they had their second child, Jill. Boy! They were two cute children! Sandy was well adjusted and had a good relationship with his dad, Walter Whitmire. Jim was in "hog heaven". He had a beautiful family and plenty of support from everyone. He knew they would "go places" eventually. Jim's wife though craved the "good life", high class society, nightclubs, attention, affluence and the like. Jim encouraged Edith to be patient, eventually everything would work out like she wanted. They were living in a house trailer at the time in a trailer park. The church was giving them ample support. Jim had become an officer of the church, and Edith was an active leader of the women of the church. Financially, life was a struggle for Jim. They had started from scratch. It was good for Jim but not Edith. One day Jim met a friend of his in the hallway of the hospital. On the spot he offered him a teaching job in a rural school in the northern part of Lakeshore County. Jim knew he wanted to go back to school. He had a good job with some prospect for the future, but he wasn't sure he wanted to go that route. He really wanted to teach as a member of a college faculty. Jim decided to change jobs and take the teaching position. Edith didn't object much; at least it was a change with some prospects. So he took a three thousand dollar or more cut in salary and walked in a classroom, untrained, to teach science in a public high school. He was on annual contract and had three years to become certified and receive a continuing contract. He went back to school, at night, on weekends, and in the summer. He had to find extra work. They couldn't live on a teacher's salary alone. Again, everyone loved them as a couple. They were sociable and active. They supported the school. They went to the dances, games and fund raising activities. Jim had many friends in the school system. He knew it was just a matter of time, he would be advanced. But in the meantime, they lived in a house trailer on a friend's lot. They had only one car. Edith did not work. She was a housewife. Jim's friend's wife and Edith sat around and thought about a better life. Jim finally bought another car to try to release her from her "prison". Finally she took a job for herself in a Ramada Inn of all places. She met a "rich" manager-owner who became overcome by her beauty and outgoing personality at the hotel. Jim had to go to the hotel and get her one night because she was intoxicated. She started running around with this manager-owner. Jim gave her a choice, either be a wife and mother for their children, or leave. She left. They got divorced, and Jim was devastated. He grieved over their children more than anything else. Jim knew clearly what opportunities for a healthy successful life his children had just lost. Jim's family and church rallied to his support. His church refused his resignation as a church officer and opened their arms out to him. He was battered but not beaten. He was down, but he got up. Jim survived, and with no hatred.

Jim's uncle Oliver Josephson who lived next door to them in the old home had a trucking business in the early days. He drove all over the local country in northwest Florida and south Alabama and bought chickens and pecans which he sold later to processing companies and retail markets. Jim would go with him often as a young boy to help drive, catch, weigh and load chickens. He was the "boss" of their family, the aggressive, authoritative influence in Jim's life. Uncle Oliver was headstrong, intelligent and possessed a stormy temper if crossed, very different from Jim's dad. He paid for his purchases from a large ledger type check book. He had a large, bold flowing signature. To Jim it was beautiful, and it "said" something about himself to everyone who saw it. Jim loved him so much. Jim remembered reflecting to himself: "I'm going to write like that one day. I am going to sign my name like that."

Chapter Three

It was that bold flowing signature on the first work order Jim had at Roy's that had caught Betsy Lee's eye that day. Jim saw her staring at it with an expression of appreciation. He always knew he had a lot more to offer her than she was aware. After his divorce Jim had obtained a pilot's license and had acquired an Advanced Ground School rating. He purchased an airplane and established a flying club. Jim and Betsy had talked about flying a lot and his job as an aviation ground school instructor. As Jim allowed things to slow down a little, he would fly over Lakeshore and out highway ninety eight when he knew she was in the shop. Jim would come in illegally low and make steep turns where she could see him. He just wanted her to know he was still around. Jim loved flying and she seemed to be interested in doing things like that, too. Jim had taken many of his students as well as many other people flying in his old piper J3 Cub, one great airplane. Jim had offered to take Betsy Lee one time, but she said Roy might object.

Jim met several other women after his divorce. One was a student of his ground school and the daughter of an airline pilot. She was a wild and crazy girl, really fun to be around. They went flying often. She enjoyed aerobatics and the wild rides Jim gave her. Jim really appreciated her confidence and trust in him as a pilot. She was in the drug culture herself, however, and Jim knew about it. She knew he wasn't into anything like that. Jim thought that was why she really liked him. He was different from the untrustworthy drug culture characters. He treated her with respect even though he knew about her involvement. She knew Jim would never become involved in anything like that and she trusted him. She was very open and told Jim about all kinds of things that were happening in the drug sub culture. One surprising thing was the people who were involved. She even told him how deliveries were made. Once Jim said to her when they were talking about these activities; "You won't get *me* to mess around with any of that stuff." She rebuffed: "You couldn't pay for it anyway." Jim realized now this was another situation that had painted him in the wrong light. People knew they were friends. He wasn't involved, though, in anything she was doing. Jim joined her dad one night at a bar and unexpectedly met another girl. They went flying some and became close friends for a short time, but this didn't last. None of those had captured his heart like Betsy Lee.

After a couple of months or so, Jim began to take his car back to Roy's for repair. She was glad to see him back around but they didn't spend a lot of time together like before. She was still interested in him. That was obvious. She had become part of his life, a part that would never really fade no matter what. Jim was there one day at the check-out counter to pay for the work they had done on his car. This was some extensive work. He had blown an engine, and they had overhauled it. Jim leaned over the counter a little and said, "Betsy, will you hand me that pen over there so I can sign this invoice? I seem to have lost mine." "Sure." She said, and reached over to pick it up from the counter. When she turned back around toward him, she said, "Jim, your collar is crooked, here let me fix it." She put down the pen, and reached up with both hands, one on each side of his collar. They were inches apart. She was so beautiful to Jim, and those blue eyes were sparking with his as she straightened his collar. She took his hand as she handed him the pen. Jim was filled with emotion. She could tell. She knew he was in love with her. Jim's heart was racing and for a brief moment as they touched, she was the fulfillment of his heart's deepest desire.

After they had moved upstairs in the apartment, Betsy's elderly mother had come to live with them. Jim had met her casually, and they had conversed. She was very receptive of Jim as though she had been expecting to meet him. She drove a white Cadillac and it stayed parked there at the shop where they lived. Jim drove up to the shop in his Volkswagen one afternoon, not long after he had the engine overhauled, and parked by the front shop door. The door was propped open. Jim's tape deck and stereo speakers were playing "The Rose". He turned off the stereo, shut the car down, got out and went through the open door of the shop. Roy, Betsy and her mother were in the shop at the time. As Jim came through the door he looked over toward Betsy and her mother and said. "Well hello, Mrs. Taylor! How are you doing today?" "I'm doing just fine." She said. Jim glanced at Betsy, and they had that nonverbal "embrace" that they almost always had. "Hi, Mrs. Harding, and how are you?" Jim asked. "I'm ok." She said. Roy was standing just in front of Jim on the other side of the counter. He turned around toward Betsy and her mother. He didn't say anything. He just stood there with his back to Jim until Betsy and Mrs. Taylor went up the stairs to the apartment above. He turned back around to Jim and said. "What can I help you with today, Mr. Josephson?" "You told me to come back about five hundred miles after the overhaul and you would change the oil and check the valves and everything. I just stopped in this afternoon to see when you could do this. It's been over five hundred miles since the overhaul." Jim said. "You have already driven that car over five hundred miles!" Roy exclaimed. "Oh yeah, it's been moving on here lately." "It must be. It hasn't been that long. I'm tied up the next day or two with work I have to get out. Bring it back next Tuesday morning and we'll take care of it for you." He said. "That will be ok. I can bring it back next Tuesday morning. I will see you next Tuesday." Jim said. "All right," Roy said. Jim went back out the open door. The upstairs apartment had a window directly above the main entry to the building. It was a narrow vertical window taller than an average person but about as wide. When Jim came out of the building, he stood there for a moment and then stepped down to open his car door. When he turned to get in, he looked up at the window. Betsy Lee was standing there in the window opening looking down, smiling and waving at him. It was a surreal moment for Jim and the emotion overcame him, but he just had to turn and leave. Roy had sent them upstairs as he came in Jim thought.

Roy left again for Mexico and for some reason her mother's car was gone. Jim thought she must have gone to Taylorville Alabama, her hometown. Betsy Lee was there because she had closed the business and her car was parked outside. Jim would never call her when she was alone, and he had never asked her to meet him anywhere. But years of these meetings and feelings had begun to pressure him to bring this to some kind of closure. Jim had not become seriously involved with anyone since he met her at the shop that day. She was the only one on his mind and in his life. Jim drove by the shop that night on his motorcycle and her car was gone. He began driving through town looking for her, but he couldn't find her anywhere. He went back by the shop where she lived and she was leaving there in her car. She crossed the east bound lane of highway 98 and stopped in the median. No cars were coming from either direction. Jim pulled up beside her window with his motorcycle. Jim pulled off his helmet, and Betsy rolled down her window. "Where are you going, Betsy?' Jim asked. "I'm going into Lakeshore to visit my sister." "Let me go with you." he asked. She knew Jim wasn't asking to go with her to her sisters. Jim had no ulterior motives, however. He just wanted to be with her. He knew they had some serious matters to resolve for her sake as well as his. "I can't let you go with me, Jim. I just can't. I don't know what Roy might do." "I'm not afraid of Roy." Jim said. "*I* am afraid of Roy." She said. "Well—ok then—I will see you again sometime." "Ok Jim, I have to go now. I will see you later." She rolled up her window, pulled out into the west bound lane headed for downtown Lakeshore. Jim was a bit let down and went out to some bars. About a week later, Jim was with Roy at the shop. He was talking to Roy, and Betsy Lee was there. Roy let Jim know, indirectly, that he knew about that incident. Jim knew Betsy Lee must have told him because no one else knew about it. Roy seemed to be letting Jim know he was in control. Jim looked over at Betsy, and she just turned away.

Jim had known this pretty young girl, Dorothy Smith, at the Credit Union for the teachers of Lakeshore County for several years. Jim visited the Credit Union often on business and he and

Dorothy would carry on friendly conversations with one another. Jim was the physics, chemistry and biology teacher for Pine Ridge High School at that time. He started dating her some because the years of not knowing and waiting for Betsy Lee to be free of Roy had amplified his need for companionship. One day Dorothy and Jim were riding on the road by his home and Betsy Lee passed by in her Cutlass Supreme and saw them together. She waved and smiled as she passed. Jim had never seen her in that part of town before, and he thought, "Uh Oh, I really didn't want that to happen." Jim really thought she might have been purposefully looking for him.

Dorothy was very responsive to Jim, and they became very close quickly. Time had taken its toll. Betsy Lee was still in his heart, but Jim thought he could read what was happening. She probably could never leave Roy while he was around whether she wanted to leave him for Jim or not. He knew too much. Roy knew by now how Jim felt, and Jim could never be sure about Betsy. She had mentioned wanting to be with Jim but never directly, always by innuendo. Jim felt she was never as emotionally involved as he was although she was strongly attracted to him physically. He didn't really know this for sure. He surely didn't want it to be true. In light of all that had happened, Jim hoped just maybe she cared for him. He wondered, based on what she had said to him, if Roy had threatened her or even himself. Jim thought at one time he was setting him up for something like that, but he was never sure. Jim was convinced Roy had made Betsy afraid to leave him under these circumstances. Besides, he knew he did not have the money and affluence that anyone Betsy would marry, would have to have. Jim also had not committed to that physical bond that indelibly clenches the love of a man and a woman. At one time, he thought he had that opportunity and had let it pass. Jim, regrettably so, had influenced her relationship with her husband and would help precipitate their separation. He knew Betsy was dissatisfied with Roy. He knew she would leave him eventually. Whatever Betsy Lee wanted to do about her marriage she couldn't do with him hanging around. Jim knew Roy would have been very angry if she had left him outright for a penniless school teacher. Roy was quite well off. Betsy Lee was responsible for most of it.

Roy drove a black Cadillac at the time, and Jim could recognize it easily. He saw it parked at a dance hall bar one night. Jim went in to see what was going on and to see if Betsy Lee was there with him. Roy was there, apparently alone, sitting at the bar. He went over and sat down on the bar stool next to him and started a conversation. Jim liked Roy and wasn't really afraid of him. They never talked about Betsy Lee. He teased Jim somewhat sarcastically about being a teacher and engaging in the bar life, alcohol and the like. He addressed him pointedly, "Teacher", his accented inflection filled with ridicule, and Jim knew what he really meant, "Womanizer". Feelings of guilt flowed through Jim's mind. Part of Roy's ridicule was because Betsy Lee was proud of Jim's accomplishments and had a lot of respect for him.

Chapter Four

J im's relationship with Dorothy grew strong. She asked him to give her a child. Jim had always wanted to have twelve children like his grandfather Josephson, so her desire to have children impressed him. Jim knew this could happen, on his part, only if they were married, and he made that clear to her. She had a previous boyfriend in Viet Nam at the time, but that didn't seem to be a problem for her. They continued to have a good relationship and Jim eventually proposed to her. The prospect of a family was very important to Jim. This had been his hope and desire with Betsy Lee. A large and loving family was always a goal in his life because his grandfather Josephson's family's love and devotion toward one another had instilled that desire in him.

Jim still wasn't sure about Betsy Lee and her intentions. It was so emotionally hard for him to let her go. Jim went back to the shop to talk to her one day, and as they talked, he asked her outright if it was ok with her if he got married. She replied quite candidly that she didn't care. It was ok with her, she said. Jim didn't detect the slightest glimmer of remorse. It was almost like she was a different person. Jim thought maybe it was a solution to the conundrum she found herself in. He was really saddened, but he didn't show it. He really wanted her to object in some way so that he would know the door was still open to him. It was a final attempt to pressure her to reveal her real feelings. Jim was really angry at himself now for acting so quickly. He knew, deep down, she cared for him. It had just been too difficult to develop a binding personal relationship. Jim's own sentiment had prevented it. Jim went away sad that day, but he knew Dorothy was committed to him and she was exciting in many ways.

Before Jim married Dorothy he went back again one day, and as he started into the shop, a man he had never seen before was leaving. When he saw Betsy, he asked her, "Who was that guy?" She replied, "He's a friend of mine, Jim. You know here lately, you have been rather personal with your questions and everything. I meet a lot of people here at the shop, and really it shouldn't be your concern." "Tell me, Betsy." Jim said. "Why did you tell Roy about the night I talked to you on the motorcycle? He let me know he knew about that. You had to tell him." She looked a little bothered about the question. "You tell me." She said. "What would have happened had he found out by himself? You know Roy. I just couldn't take that chance." "Well Betsy—I may as well go on—you are not going anywhere. I don't know when I will see you again. You take care of yourself." "Yes Jim—I will—I will see you again, I guess, sometime."

Jim was more than a little bothered about this conversation. For so many years they had been such very close friends. She knew he had more than just a little interest in her. She knew Jim was really in love with her. Her friend appeared to be an accomplished person. Jim had a feeling he was an affluent business man. Jim could see the hand writing on the wall, and he knew it was over. It had been an incredible journey for him, and Jim would never be the same. Just six months after Jim married Dorothy, he learned Betsy and Roy had divorced and she had left Roy for good. Jim knew his actions had opened the door for her. He didn't know the details because he had not seen her since they had parted that last day. Roy would never let her safely leave while he was in the picture, whether her interest in him was real or imagined. They were too deeply involved in questionable activities for Roy to take that chance, he believed. He felt Roy never really knew for sure if he was an agent or not.

Jim had written a creative writing for her as their relationship had grown, expressing his feelings. He intended to give it to her because he wanted her to know what was really in his heart. Jim was never able to talk to her openly about his deepest feelings. Outwardly Jim thought she perceived him to be a person who would approach a woman just to satisfy the moment. She didn't seem too uncomfortable with that view of a man. Once she had said she thought his deep fascination with her was because she was someone he couldn't attain easily. A few people had that view of Jim. Some thought he was a promiscuous person. Even his Principal friend did, because he asked Jim outright one time. Jim attracted the attention of a lot of women. Women were drawn to him like a magnet it seemed, but Jim was not a trivial or promiscuous person. Sometime later Jim saw her with her mother at a beauty shop near the house where he and Dorothy lived at the time. This was the first time he had seen her since she left Roy. When he greeted her he said: "You rascal!" in a half joking manner, alluding to her quick divorce after his marriage. She was startled at that and looked bewildered. Evidently she did not make the connection he anticipated and that made him wonder about his rationalizations. Jim talked with them for a brief period and as they started to leave, Jim told Betsy to wait a moment, he had something that was hers. He stepped inside his home to get it and when he came out, he gave her the creative writing. They parted cordially, and Betsy and her mother left together in her mother's white Cadillac.

A few months after that, Jim began to look for her again and finally found her working in a real estate office. He went to see her. He talked to her briefly and learned that she had taken some trips (He supposed, with this man he had seen) on a yacht to the Bahamas or somewhere around Florida. She was doing ok and looked good, but she was not the radiant lady that he once knew. Jim asked her to meet with him (isn't that ironic, he was married now and she was single!). Jim asked her to go out to dinner with him. He wanted to talk and to really let her know what had happened to him. She said no, she couldn't handle anything like that now knowing he was married. Jim said goodbye, held back his grief, and left. Jim drove down Highway Ninety eight in Lakeshore and passed by Roy's old Volkswagen shop. He looked up into the window in the shop, and in the memory of his mind a scene of times past came to view. He could see her there, smiling and waving, and he knew he loved her. Regretfully, he thought, she never knew how much he really loved her. Jim wondered what life would have been had he kissed her that day.

The next day Jim returned to the school where he taught. He sat at his desk in his classroom where so many students had shared their lives and ambitions with him. He thought about the trust and confidence they had placed in him and how they valued his advice and counseling when they were faced with a difficult situation or decision. He loved those students, and the rapport he generated with them had come through genuine caring, concern and fairness for every student regardless of their station in life or their personal problems. Jim was an unspoken leader among the student body of his school.

He put his head in his hands and began to reflect on his own ambitions and goals and what had unfolded in his life in the last few years. He realized his own reputation among some of the leaders of the community and school system had been tarnished by his questionable activity as they had viewed it. His chances for a leadership role in his school and school district were nil due to his scientific views about evolution and the progressive democratic political views he held about government in general. He was viewed as a liberal democrat among a sea of conservative republicans and fundamentalist Christians. The majority of the republican leaders had once been his democratic friends but had converted to the conservative republican philosophy mainly because of social issues and fundamentalist Christian views. Jim watched as they were fed a continuous anti government propaganda by the NRA, businesses' anti EPA stance, and hard right fundamentalist Christians concerned about prayer in schools and the teaching of evolutionary principles in the public schools. Nationally, Republicans used taxes as their modus operandi to further alienate the voters from programs that were meant to benefit the working class. Even before Ruby Ridge the NRA leadership took a pro militia, anti law enforcement (BATF), anti-government stance, and denigrated elected officials, sitting presidents and anyone else that approved of any gun control measure. Jim could see how the NRA leadership influenced conservative groups, religious and otherwise, to take up the anti-government posture in their attempt to air their views. All of this to Jim just amplified the division and lack of brotherhood in the Congress of the United States. Jim had always supported the right to bear arms. His collector's license and large gun collection was ample witness for that. He was disgusted by the approach the NRA leaders had taken because they had created so much distrust in so many leaders that were really working for the good of the people. Jim's moral and ethical views were Christian just like the majority of theirs but they thought they had reason to believe otherwise. Jim became acutely aware of the effect of his views when one of his friends had commented, concerning leadership positions, "You just couldn't be trusted."

Jim straightened up and opened the old Macintosh computer sitting on his desk. This was the one he used to process all of his lesson plans, records, and other school work at the school. It had a large desktop full of folders, one for each general area of work. He ran down the list of folders until he came to one labeled "Personal". This was the folder where he kept many of his personal files. Inside he found a folder labeled "Reflections". Moving down to a file labeled "To Betsy" Jim opened the file and began reading to himself.

To Betsy

When in those special moments I meet you,
I see the beauty of a pretty smile,
And from your glowing radiant face
Your sparkling eyes reach out
And greet with warm embrace.

And in that moment,
In the twinkling starlight of your eyes,
I see the spring time of earth pass by,
With all the fragrance of its woodland flowers in full bloom.
For as the mystic magic of your eyes meet mine,
I feel the power of our earth's eternal spring
Flowing like a fountain, from within, unseen.

I see the towering timber on the rolling hills of earth,
And walk beneath the boughs of brown and gold and green,
I hear the whispering wind from off the
mountain peaks come down,
And watch the lofty eagle soar among the clouds,
And from the depths of earth I feel a moving spirit flow,
And watch the earth unfold in scenes of wondrous joy.

And if, perchance, someday, my dreams come true,
It's sure that all the earth would only bloom to me
In flowers of spring!

Chapter Five

J im and Dorothy have had a good life together, even though they have opposite views about many things and are opposites in many aspects of their personalities. They have reared two wonderful boys; Joseph and Samuel. At the present time, March the first two thousand and seven, Joseph is a graduate student in history at the University of West Florida and Samuel is a senior at the University of Central Florida in Orlando. He will graduate Summa Cum Laude in Civil Engineering this spring. Jim and Dorothy satisfied each other's need for intimate companionship, but the emotional bonding was weaker since they viewed many aspects of life differently. Jim worked hard to provide everything she needed as well as emotional support because she is quick to anger and very defensive. Dorothy is very attractive and well endowed with long flowing brown hair and a beautiful smile. She is very outgoing in some ways and loves to play games, work puzzles and compete with others on the internet. Had Jim been a young man, (she was twenty two, and he was forty one when they married) it would have been very difficult for them to work out their differences. Having already been there once, Jim was willing to compromise his own particular demands about many things and just let them ride in order to make things go smoothly and keep the family together. Jim concentrated on the good things they experienced together and just let the others ride. Jim's mother had advised him to do this. His Mother knew Jim demanded perfection in almost everything and that would have to change. One good thing happened as they adjusted to each other's differences. Jim quit drinking beer at home on a regular basis because he knew beer and Dorothy would make adjusting very difficult. She knows the difficulty he has with her, and she lets him know that she deeply loves him and appreciates what he does for her. That is a great plus for Jim. Jim and Dorothy have had many good times with her families and friends and he has come to love them very much. Her natural parents were divorced early in their marriage and have remarried more than once. All of them are very good to him and treat him with the utmost respect, even though he is about the same age as her parents. One time her grandmother Smith (her natural father's mother) came to stay with Jim and Dorothy for a while. She was a country lady, and Jim had developed a good relationship with her from the very beginning. She loved Dorothy very much. She became acutely aware of Dorothy's temperament during this stay. Grandmother and Jim would work together picking and shelling vegetables and doing other chores and just have a great time. Often they would talk about old times and her life as a child. But just the added stress of her presence, although Dorothy loved her grandmother dearly, made Dorothy's behavior very difficult for both of them in the routine of every-day life. Grandmother Smith said to Jim one day after some difficult interactions, "Son, I just don't know what makes Dorothy be like that". Jim replied: "Well Grandma, I will take care of her for you. Don't you worry. I will take care of her."

Jim never forgot Betsy Lee. He had partitioned the hard drive, to use a modern phrase. Dorothy was the one in his life and he loved her, but he had a place in his heart that only Betsy Lee occupied. Often he would journey through the country, down the old roads and through the old towns that he and his Uncle Oliver had visited years ago. He would visit the old woodland places where he had so many great times hunting and fishing with his Dad and Uncle Oliver. This would always refresh him and fill him with righteous feelings of meaningful purpose. During some of those times of reflection, he would remember again his relationship with Betsy Lee, and contemplate again those memories of someone he still loved very much. Occasionally he would go to Taylorville where she grew up, to visit the place where she had lived. Jim didn't try to keep track of her. He just kept thoughts of her from completely fading from his memory. Jim asked Roy a couple of times about her, but he would always be very vague and not really tell him anything. Jim really thought she had left this general area and didn't know for sure where she was. Once when Jim was in Taylorville, He decided to ask around about her and her family. He drove down the main street of Taylorville and saw an older man working in front of an old hotel. Jim stopped and started a conversation with him about the old buildings and the town. The older gentleman responded very positively and began to tell him everything he knew about the old town. Jim asked him about Betsy Lee and her family. He remembered her and began to tell Jim what he could remember about them. He told Jim where her brother lived, and Jim made a note of it in his check book. Jim asked him about the old place he had encountered years ago with her maiden name on the mailbox. He said: "No, those Taylors were not her people. They were colored folks." Jim had to catch himself to keep from laughing out loud. "That girl!" He exclaimed to himself. She had pulled a good one on him and he never knew it at the time. When he asked her about the place, she had said: "Probably where one of your girl friends lived." Jim had been fooled and didn't know it. He wondered at the time why she was laughing so at him.

Once he stopped by the Volkswagen place just to see Roy. He was there with this woman that Jim assumed to be his girlfriend. They talked a little about this and that. The woman became very friendly with Jim. When he started to leave they offered him a drink. They were both drinking tequila, he thought. Jim said sure and had a couple of drinks just before he left. Boy! He didn't know what was in those drinks, but it wasn't just alcohol. He got a kick out of that he had never experienced before. The lady was already interested in him, and he began to be interested in her. He knew he had better get out of there quick. He left and that was the last time he ever saw Roy again.

Chapter Six

When Dorothy and Jim met, Jim had quit going to church. He hadn't attended church since he had first met Betsy Lee. His mother and aunt were devout Presbyterians, and they had overseen all of his church activity as he grew up. Jim's father seldom went to church and was not a member. He and Jim's Uncle Oliver usually went fishing or hunting, or went to visit their brothers on Sunday mornings. His Mother, though, demanded that he go to church. As Jim grew older he came to enjoy the social activities of the Church and didn't mind going. He always had a love for the writings of the bible. Jim loved the Psalms and Isaiah probably the most. He read a lot from the Bible and commentary, but he formed his own opinions. Jim questioned a lot of the fundamental beliefs that established some of Christianity's most important doctrines. The teachings of Jesus, though, were very profound and moving to Jim particularly, in the Gospel of John, and the other books of John. After reading and studying the writings over many years, he came to have a deep and personal embrace with the heart of Jesus' teaching. Some of his mentors and teachers in his younger years had wanted him to become a minister. Jim had considered this but he had too many unanswered questions and knew no one was going to be able answer them satisfactorily but himself. During his first marriage he had served as an officer of the church. Jim was a good speaker, a good leader, could sing well, loved the songs of the church, and had what some people said was charisma. Dorothy asked him outright before they were married if he would go to church with her. Jim said he would, and they started attending the Lakeshore Presbyterian Church where he had his membership. Jim's first son

Aaron and his daughter, Jill, had been born to his first wife Edith when they were members of this church. Dorothy gave birth to Joseph while they attended there and was pregnant with another child. One of the elders of the church jokingly asked Jim one day: "Jim, what are you going to name this one? Moses?" Well, they named him Samuel. Dorothy was active and participated in many activities. Jim became very active and eventually became Chairman of the Board of Deacons. He sang bass in the church choir. Jim was to be considered for Elder when Dorothy had a misunderstanding with some of the members and refused to attend this church any longer. Jim could have continued with his responsibilities there, but it would have meant splitting a family's worship experience and Jim wouldn't do that. Dorothy absolutely refused to go back to that church. No amount of persuading would change her mind. Jim knew he could not force her to do it. One couldn't force her to do anything, even something superficial. Jim was a little dissatisfied with the way the difficulty had been handled. He was not consulted. If he had been, he could have resolved it without the hard feelings, and no one would have quit. It was as if they didn't really want him to resolve it even though it was his wife and he was Chairman of the Board of Deacons. Jim changed churches with Dorothy. Jim had many friends in the church he left and really didn't believe what Dorothy was forcing him to do was what he should do. Having one split family, though, was enough. Jim would not have another one. They moved to a Baptist church. One of the members of his former church asked him one day, "You lost a part of yourself when you left that church didn't you Jim?" Jim replied dejectedly, "Yes, I did."

Jim made many new friends in the new Baptist church they joined. The choir needed help, and Jim helped make it a happy choir that the congregation enjoyed greatly. Jim loved the people who attended there. The majority were working class folks that Christ had loved so much. Some relatives of Jim's father's family were there, and it was a joy for him to be there with them. Jim's sons joined the church there, and Jim was baptized with them according to the Baptist Church's tradition. Jim was again nominated to be an officer of the church. Dorothy was engaged in the women's work and many other activities. Then, one day, it happened again. Something offended Dorothy, and she quit again. She absolutely refused to go back to that church. Everyone tried to dissuade her to no avail. Deacons came to Jim's home and literally begged her to stay. She would not. She never divulged to Jim the reason she had wanted to quit, but it involved the preacher at the church. Regretfully to Jim they changed churches again. This time they changed to an affluent church with a moderately large membership. The church had a great pastor, a real lover of Christ and His church. He was a conservative fundamentalist as most southern Baptist ministers in the area are. Jim explained to Dorothy he wasn't changing churches anymore after this. Jim decided not to take a leadership part in this church for two reasons. First, Jim didn't want to get established and have another incident disrupt his work or the activities of the church. Secondly, Jim was a science teacher and over the years he had come to reject some fundamentalists views of the scripture and some of the doctrines and platforms those views supported. Jim had also come to strongly reject any active involvement in partisan politics by the organized Church.

After becoming a teacher, Jim had plenty of time to read and study. Jim read everything about science he could comprehend while also reading secular literature and research about the origin and history of the Christian Church. Long ago Jim had made it one of his goals to investigate the controversies between science and religion and to see if he could contribute in some small way to resolutions and enlightenment in both domains. Jim had also read and re-read the Bible and continued to read the Bible in various versions. Jim had heavy, one way written discussions with a brilliant Jewish, atheist Harvard paleontologist who loved mankind and all of nature. He was the author of a standing column "This View of Life" in Natural History magazine. Jim had corresponded with him about several of his writings that appeared in this column. The professor respected other peoples' right to religious views but actively rebutted their world view when it conflicted with established scientific principles. All of this activity precluded any real leadership role in this very conservative fundamentalist church, and Jim knew it. Jim considered joining the choir, but Dorothy didn't want him to join. She wanted Jim to sit with her, now that they were in a new church.

Jim loved the worship. The religious songs of his childhood, great music, great preaching (Jim disregarded the fundamentalist emphasis), and a beautiful atmosphere and sanctuary, just filled Jim with joy. His heart was filled with the spirit and love of Christ he had experienced through his family at home and through the moving power of the written scriptures of the Old and New Testaments of the Bible.

During this time, Joseph and Samuel were attending private Christian School even though Jim was a public high school teacher. Joseph and Samuel are loved and respected by everyone they meet. They are courteous and kind to everyone. They participated in school athletics (mostly basketball, a little track) through school. They lettered in basketball, and Samuel was the highest average scorer in Lakeshore County his senior year. Jim and Dorothy had a great time working with their boys and supporting the academic and athletic programs there. Jim helped coach his younger son's final Gospel Projects baseball team through a championship season. They both were Florida Merit Scholars and had their college tuition paid by the State of Florida.

Jim's older children were very close to him. He had supported them every way he could and had the respect and support of their step father. The broken relationship, however, took its toll. His beautiful and intelligent daughter had married before finishing high school, and his son married shortly thereafter. They had six children between them, three each, but both marriages failed. They were always struggling financially, and Jim was always trying to help the best he could. After the death of Jim's parents, Jim allowed Aaron, his oldest son, to live in the old home of his childhood. Both Aaron and Jill lived there with his parents for a year once while their mother recuperated from a serious illness. Both of them came to love his parents dearly during this time with them. They gave them the love and support they had given Jim because they were just great parents and were filled with real love and kindness. This experience had a profound effect on Aaron, and he loved them and the old place dearly. Aaron has since remarried and is beginning to have a good life. Jill, bless her heart, is still struggling. She has difficulty making the right choices for a life partner. Jill has a big heart like her dad, and it gets hurt easily by people who don't respect what she does for them.

This was the family Jim brought to Lakeview Baptist Church when they joined there. Dorothy and Jim were in the same couple's class for several years. They had good fellowship there and met many new people. After some time they decided to separate and attend separate classes. Jim did not attempt to sing in the choir in honor of Dorothy's request, although he really wanted to sing. They sang in the church services of course and on Wednesday night. They didn't attend often on Sunday night. Jim worked every other weekend on Sunday night at Bayview Memorial Hospital as he had for many years. Wednesday nights were special. A family supper was sponsored by the church previous to the Wednesday night prayer meeting. At first, Jim's entire family attended this Wednesday night supper, including three of his grandchildren. Dorothy eventually decided to stop attending, because of weight concerns, and so did Lynn and Matt, two of his grandchildren. Joseph and Samuel began to have college classes and meetings so their attendance became sporadic. Franklin, Jim's older son's youngest child, continued to attend with Jim faithfully. After the supper, Jim would always go early to the sanctuary to read the bible or other related literature. The minister of music first led singing before the prayer meeting started. This was one of Jim's special times because he loved to sing the old church songs. Jim was burdened with extensive hearing loss due to airplane engines, guns and a condition in his left ear known as Meniere's disease. It was relatively quiet at this time, and Jim could sing out because he could hear better.

Many professionals attended this church including school teachers and leaders of the Lakeshore County School System. Jim knew many of them. His county science supervisor was one of them.

Jim noticed how many beautiful and elegant ladies were members of the church. They always dressed just beautifully and had so much sophistication and poise. Jim knew how easily he could become attracted to beautiful women. Jim was a handsome and charismatic man with many talents and abilities and had a magnetic appeal to most of the women he met. Jim tried to exemplify everyone's reason for being at church and not let any of these kinds of influences enter into the worship activities.

After several years of attendance, Jim joined the older men's class and really enjoyed studying the bible with them. Jim always admired older men for their maturity and wisdom. He had grown up being around older men most of the time. One of the men, T. W. Bishop, was very charismatic and knowledgeable about the bible and its teaching. He was a very emotional person and Jim liked him very much. He and his wife Jacquelyn and his son's and daughter's families were actively involved in church activities. Jim's father had passed away not long before he became a member of the men's class. This was a great loss to Jim. Jim mentioned to T. W. once that he had come to the older men's class looking for a spiritual father. As their friendship grew Jim began to look on T. W. as his spiritual father. Jim's nephew's father in law, Mr. Joel, was also a member of this class. He was a member of the old hunting party of Jim's father's family. Mr. Joel was another reason Jim had decided to attend the older men's class.

Jim came to know his "spiritual father" quite well and he and his wife, Jacquelyn, became very close friends of his. Jim had noticed their daughter, Angela Davis, when he was trying to learn who people were in the church and learn their names. She was much younger than Jim and was married to a nice looking young man, Mark Davis. They taught a Sunday school class as a couple. They had three daughters. On first meeting, Angela and Jim had introduced themselves to each other and he had learned she was an elementary school teacher. She was a very attractive young lady and projected some of the emotional attributes that were characteristic of her father. Jim thought to himself at the time, "I surely don't want anything to happen between the two of us. She is Mr. Bishop's daughter, and I wouldn't want anything in the world to come between us." Jim knew how easy it was for amorous relationships between him and attractive women to develop. Those kinds of relationships with Jim, though, were almost totally dependent on a woman's initiative. Jim saw several of the ladies noticing him from time to time. He returned their glances; it was just his nature, but Jim didn't try to promote anything. He was very cautious. He behaved like the Christian gentleman he had always tried to be. He loved this church, and didn't want to become a stumbling block for anyone. Jim also wanted to be straightforward and honest. He had presented a written letter to the officers of the church outlining his views about evolution and science so that everyone would know how he stood on those issues.

Jim talked often with Angela and one of her friends before Wednesday night suppers. Angela and her friend were both elementary school teachers at the same school. Jim met them from time to time in the serving line. They never sat together, however. Jim sat with his family in the beginning. He sat occasionally with some of the other members. Jim knew many of them. Some of them had been his students of science in the public school. Angela, her friends and their husbands, and sometimes other younger couples sat in front of him in the Wednesday night prayer meetings. They would sing hymn book songs and songs from the church choir literature. Jim would sing out with emotion and express the deep spiritual feelings he held inside. Sometimes Jim would sing the bass parts with strong inflection of tone to express deep emotion. He really enjoyed doing this and occasionally after the songs you would hear the, amen, of approval for the deep feelings the songs were generating within the congregation. Many times Jim was asked to join the choir. Jim realized that Angela was noticing his singing. She was turning to look at him from time to time. She was a choir member. Her husband sat beside her. Jim could never hear him singing though.

In the morning service at church, when Jim could, his hearing was so bad, he would sing with the same Wednesday night enthusiasm. Jim would look at the members of the choir often as they sang and express his emotional exhilaration and feeling because Jim really had a spiritual "high" in his heart. Jim admired the sophistication and grace that many of the ladies had. He really appreciated them and felt *spiritually* uplifted by their character and participation. The beautiful mosaic cross behind the choir would transmit colored light down across the members and beams of light would shine through the tinted side windows. It was as if the Light of Christ was shining throughout the sanctuary, Christ's light of love. Jim had always had visions for a better world. He could hear Isaiah crying out his vision of hope for his people and the people of the world. Jim could see Christ fulfilling that vision as the suffering servant to an impoverished and suffering world. The Biblical hope for a better world also filled Jim's spirit and his emotions poured forth in worship. Jim was acutely aware of the state of affairs on the earth. Regretfully aware of the starving and impoverished people in other parts of the world and the affluence our people enjoyed. He was acutely aware of the biological, ecological and social crisis that the earth and mankind were in. He was overwhelmed at the prospects of war and death in a "holy" land, and the scourge of disease and pestilence going unchecked. Jim knew about the challenges to religious belief that new knowledge and understanding was bringing to an imprisoned religious audience of fundamentalism and the effect it might have on their faith and our societies. He was acutely aware of the political divisions in the Country and Christianity's questionable engagement. He realized new perspectives and enlightenments would need to be formulated by the spiritually enlightened to maintain the credibility of the Christian Church in the scientific world of the twentieth and twenty first centuries. He was filled with spiritual vision and purpose. Jim always had been. The Church with its congregation of worshipers, beautiful sanctuary, music and dynamic preaching amplified those visions with sincere feelings and deep emotion.

Chapter Seven

There was a period of casual interest for several years between Angela and Jim, but it was like any other Christian friendship that one would have. It happened one Wednesday night at the supper when they were standing in the serving line. Jim was in front of her waiting to get served. He turned around and Angela was standing right behind him in the line. When their eyes met she just filled with deep emotion. She turned away quickly, apparently embarrassed at her own reaction. Jim knew in that instant, in that moment, they had shared an emotional experience. Jim's relationship with her had always been as a Christian friend. Jim had not even thought about any other kind of relationship. She was T. W. Bishop's daughter, and he had already decided to not let anything happen between them. He never thought too much about it. He was not interested in pursuing her attention in any sensual manner, both were married. He hardly knew her. Evidently it had more impact on her than Jim expected. She must have had strong feelings of guilt and betrayal. She came to the altar at the end of church service several times during this period. Jim noticed some changes in her relationship with her husband and thought he was watching to see if he made any advances or anything. He stopped sitting with her in the prayer meeting session. Jim noticed him sitting over on the back row one night, possibly watching him to see if he made any advances or anything. Jim began to think she might have said something about their encounter to someone, maybe even her husband. Jim had tried to talk to Angela, but each time the conversation was brief and he had no opportunity to rectify the situation. One day Jim needed to go over to her dad's house to get some literature. He went at a time when he thought Angela might be there so he could talk this thing out a little while her dad was present and clear the air of any intent on his part. Sure enough, Angela came there with her children after school was out. She came through the room he and her dad were in, made a short greeting, glanced at Jim's physical self in a rebuking manner, and went zipping out. Jim thought: "Uh oh, no talking here. I won't be able to solve anything here."

One Sunday not long after that had transpired, Dorothy and Jim attended Sunday school. They met in the sanctuary for assembly. After the assembly was dismissed, Jim started down the hallway toward the Older Men's class. Weaving his way through the crowded hallway, he met Jacquelyn Bishop, Angela's mother, in front of her classroom door. "Well hello, Mrs. Bishop. How are you today? It's good to see you." Jim said. "I'm doing well today, considering those old headaches I have been having. I don't have one today. How are you doing? I heard you've been having some difficulty lately. You need to go see a doctor before it gets out of hand." She replied. "Oh, I just have ear trouble. I have Meniere's in my left ear. I have it under control now. I work in the laboratory at Bayview Memorial, so I can keep an eye on my ear." Jim laughed. She laughed with him and said: "You take good care of yourself now and stay out of trouble." "Ok, Mrs. Bishop. I'll sure do that." Jim thought. Stay out of trouble? Jim wondered what in the world she meant by that. Was she talking about Angela and him? Jim was bothered about this. He went on down to the Older Men's classroom. The door was shut. Everyone was probably already there. Many of the older men went straight to their classroom and did not go to assembly. Jim opened the door and stepped inside. Mr. Joel, Jim's nephew's father-in-law, was sitting just to his right counting the collection. "Hi there, Mr. Joel, how are you doing?" Jim asked as he handed him his offering. "Oh, I am doing ok, Mr. Jim." He said. Jim turned to the rest of them seated around the walls and said: "Hello, everyone!" They all greeted him warmly. Several of the men spoke up and one said: "Come on in. We are glad to have you. There's a chair right over here." T. W. looked up from his desk, he was the teacher. He didn't say anything, and he didn't have a very inviting look on his face. Jim sat down, and he began with that

Sunday's lesson. T. W. is a good teacher. He engages everyone in the discussions and makes it interesting. Toward the end of the lesson, he began to discuss matters of the Church. "Well, we have had some complaints about objectionable behavior lately, concerning people's eye contact." He looked over at Jim as he continued. "Someone has been coming on to others by their eye contact. This is just completely inappropriate behavior in a Church." He was looking straight at Jim when he said it, and his look wasn't very pleasing. He hadn't mentioned any names and the other members did not know what he was talking about, but Jim did, and T. W. knew it. Jim spoke up and said: "You know that works both ways, T. W." "Oh no," He said. "Others in the choir have also complained about people's eye contact, and it makes them feel uneasy." "Well." Jim said. "The Bible says, T. W., if there is a misunderstanding between two people, they should meet together with officers of the Church and resolve it." "Oh no, that would just turn into a blaming game with each party claiming that God was on their side. I know what will happen. The instigating party will just ignore it and let it pass on by, just as if nothing had ever happened." By now some of the other members of the class were catching on to what was going on. He was angry, and Jim could tell it. There went Jim's spiritual dad.

After that, Jim really watched his step and kept his distance. Jim had no real serious interest in pursuing this. He loved Angela's mother and father very much. He just wanted everyone, particularly Angela, to worship in peace and be happy. This, however, was not to happen. The encounter had sparked deep emotion in Angela and she could not stop looking at Jim and he could not stop returning her glances. It was more than just amorous attraction. It involved the singing of the hymns, the deep spirituality of the church and seemingly to Jim, some kind of background religious experience that Angela had encountered that was unknown to Jim. He thought about entrapment but could not believe that it was present in her communication with him. One time after a Wednesday night service, the minister of music walked by the pew where Jim was sitting and remarked kind of sarcastically, "Congratulations," and just kept going. Jim thought:

"My goodness, what does he mean?" Jim had a feeling he knew why he had said this. Jim thought Angela and her husband might have been having marital problems and he was blaming him in some way. The minister of music had been promoting her husband in various activities in the Church. He had also stopped leading Wednesday night singing just before prayer meeting, one part of worship Jim really enjoyed. Jim wondered if the Minister of Music had done this because of his relationship with Angela. Jim wondered if the Minister of Music thought he had other reasons for being there. Jim knew he had not intentionally instigated anything in the Church to promote a relationship with Angela.

The feelings between Jim and Angela just kept growing and they could not avoid them. Their attraction began to be obvious to other people. Jim was sitting with his family during one night service and he and Angela were exchanging glances as often happened. It was very conspicuous this time on her part because she was sitting in front of Jim and had to turn around in the pew and look back to see him. It was obvious to anyone noticing, that she had an emotional interest in Jim. As she turned toward Jim and their eyes met in an emotional exchange, Jim felt like he heard the words, "I love you", spoken. He was startled because he had not consciously said those words. Jim said to himself, "My goodness, I didn't say that!" Jim looked around at those around him but no one was speaking to him. Jim thought, "Good grief! This is not happening to us is it?", because he knew the heartache it was going to cause for him. Jim wrestled with this strange happening for weeks before he realized that he could not deny what was happening to him, though he tried hard to do so. It was almost as if they were having an emotional mind meld and could communicate from a distance. They shared, spiritually, many of the activities during Church services from a distance. Jim thought they both were experiencing the effects of a deep spiritual relationship. Her eyes were beginning to touch Jim's heart, like Betsy Lee's had done so many years ago, even though Jim had tried to avoid it.

Not long after some of these experiences, Jim had a dream. Jim dreamed Angela was sleeping at his feet. She moved toward him in her sleep, and when she did her hair touched Him. When it did, a peace flowed over Jim, one like he had never experienced before. It was like a deep spiritual compassion was there. The dream ended as abruptly as it had begun. When Jim awoke, He remembered it vividly. Jim pondered over this dream for several days, knowing that it wasn't something he had done, but something Angela had done that had brought this feeling of spiritual peace to him in the dream. It was a puzzle. Jim had the general feeling that she had fallen in love with him. She would never withdraw her emotion regardless of the attention it was gathering. Then one day, the similarity to a biblical incident dawned on Jim; Ruth sleeping at the feet of Boaz. Jim thought, "Why would my mind initiate such a dream?" He was very concerned about this. He kept trying to deny his feelings to himself because he thought in his heart, as he had before, it was wrong. Jim actually loved her Christian husband as a brother. This gift had been given to Jim. It was easy for Jim to love with the agape love of the Christian faith.

One day, when Jim was riding in the country, he began thinking about what was happening between Angela and him. He realized then he was beginning to be caught up in another emotional experience that was getting really serious. Her emotional persistence had been too strong. No one would believe that Jim was really the vulnerable one. A powerful sexual drive and a profusion of emotion gave the world a dazzling aura where visions of righteousness interplayed with moments of desire. Jim knew the heartbreak he was about to experience and the hard decisions he would have to make.

In another dream, Jim and Angela's mother were riding in a car together. Jim was sitting in the back seat. Jacquelyn reached over from the front seat and handed Jim her husband's bible. The second dream was as abrupt as the first one. Jim wondered again, "Why would I have such a dream as this?" Jim pondered what all of this really meant. Out of it had come conflicting views by various people, deep misunderstandings by some, unresolved heartaches, and unknown intents. Jim loved his wife and family and knew he would not forsake them, but could not deny his feelings.

Chapter Eight

Throughout all of Jim's thirty five years of teaching science in the public school, he had worked part time every other weekend in a hospital laboratory. For many years he worked at the County General Hospital in Lakeshore, Florida. General Hospital was a county owned hospital that cared for the indigent and needy. After many years of part time work there, the county closed this facility, and Jim was hired to work at Bayview Memorial. He became friends with several coworkers during this time. When he retired from teaching, they increased his work time to half time, so Jim could receive benefits. One of the girls working there had been converted to Christianity, and they often talked about religious concerns and matters of their faith. A young Vietnamese technologist also worked with them. He was of the Buddhist inclination. Jim often talked to him about their spiritual and religious viewpoints. Jim expressed his feelings about the exclusion that accompanied the narrow fundamentalist view of Christianity and explained to him that he did not hold those views. Jim had read from most of the eastern religious literature and had become familiar with some of the writings of Buddhism. Their discussions became quite heavy, and Jim expressed some of his deepest concerns about the direction Fundamentalist Christianity was taking. He expressed his reverence for some of the Buddhist passages from their literature and even read one to him, relating it to the Christian views that Jim held. When he saw Jim's acceptance, openness and rejection of the exclusion fundamentalist views projected, he began to accept Jim completely and they became best friends.

The hospital had an intern program and many young students come to study medical laboratory science there. One of the students (Nancy Neilson) and Jim became especially close friends as they worked together in the laboratory. Nancy was very friendly and always responded with a beautiful smile. In the beginning she worked as an accessioner, handling the specimens and orders that arrived in the laboratory. Eventually Nancy came to work in Jim's department as a coworker. They worked together well and became close friends. She and the young Vietnamese technologist shared many of Jim's views about science and religion, and they too questioned the fundamentalist's narrow and dogmatic views about creation and evolution.

Nancy and Jim talked about animals often. They both had cats and she had a talking crow at home. Jim always felt animals had more intelligence and understanding than scientists gave them. She agreed with him and they shared some of the experiences they had communicating with their pets. They had dinner together often at the hospital in the beginning. Eventually Jim realized their relationship was becoming a little too personal. Reflecting on what was happening in his life; Jim realized he needed to proceed with caution. They agreed to be "just friends". She and the young Vietnamese Technologist came to dine with Jim and Dorothy at his home once. He was a billiards player. Jim has a pool table at home, and they enjoyed a few games of pool. To Jim they have been an uplifting influence on his life in a difficult time. They have treated him with such great respect and caring. Some in the laboratory do not hold the same views Jim has about science and religion. They have never wavered though in their support and respect for Jim and his work. They have been, and always will be his friends.

Jim came to work at the laboratory once and as he entered the work room two or three of his friends were standing around a new employee laughing and talking. They introduced her to Jim as Mary Duncan and they greeted each other. She looked at Jim and said, "Can I kiss you? She (meaning one of Jim's fiends there) wouldn't let me kiss her." Jim replied laughingly, "Sure, come on. I don't mind if you kiss me." She kissed Jim on the cheek and said to the other girl, "He let me kiss him, why wouldn't you let me kiss you?" Jim spoke up and said, "I know why she wouldn't let you kiss her." Mary asked, "Why?" Jim replied, "Because she is a girl and I am a man." They all laughed about this and Mary became his close friend. They often embraced when they met each other. They went to dinner together often and talked a lot about both of their lives. She had been through difficulty and divorce also. Jim was able to open up to her and talk about all of the things that were happening to him at church. He asked for her opinion and advice. Mary said quite frankly, "It's the devil, Jim you need to move on and never look back." Jim replied sternly, "Mary, I have heard enough about this Satan stuff lately, I don't believe in an independent spirit flitting around trying to disrupt people's lives. I think what we call "evil" exists within one's own self because of the choices that we make and the nature of our expectations for ourselves that we establish through our experiences in life." She replied quizzically, "You don't believe in the devil?" Jim said, "No, not as an entity itself." She admonished, "Devil or not, you need to move on. It doesn't appear that anything good can come out of this for either one of you, two broken marriages? All of the children?" Jim explained how much relief it was just to be able to talk to her, since he had not even touched the other lady and no one would talk to him directly about it. Jim thought it was very interesting that she appeared in his life at this particular time and was also named Mary. Mary and Jim had no intimate relations with each other. Contrary to what some people might have thought, Jim was not that kind of person and never had been. They embraced each other but they were just friends. Jim wrote her a written account of his encounter at church and sent it to her by e-mail. She had approved this. They thought he might need it one day. They remained good friends. She eventually changed jobs, and Jim lost close contact with her except for an occasional e-mail.

Jim kept Mary's advice in mind. He knew it was good advice and really what Jim had accepted himself, but the emotion was powerful. Jim had always been a visionary. He had started to wonder what life with her might be like. He had a deep need to share his spiritual aspirations with a companion he loved. Jim was almost seventy years old, though, and Angela did not know this. How could she feel this relationship could possibly be good for her in the long run, he wondered? What were her real intentions? Jim could never really believe she was just seeking a physical relationship. It was even more difficult for him to believe it was entrapment.

Chapter Nine

J im didn't know if Dorothy knew anything at this point, but she was always letting Jim know she loved him and cared for him. Once she asked Jim spontaneously, "Jim, you are not going to leave me, are you?" Jim replied, "Goodness no, Dorothy, I am not going to leave you. Why would I want to leave you?" She made no reply that answered that question, and the conversation changed to another subject. Jim thought then she might know what was happening between him and Angela. Dorothy and Jim adjusted well with married life even though they have differences in personality and opinions. Who really doesn't? They have had great times together. Jim hasn't had problems at home other than their somewhat conflicting personalities, and Jim had mentioned this to Angela's father.

In Church in the morning services Angela and Jim would engage emotionally as inspiring parts of the service unfolded and could almost talk to each other it seemed. Jim tried to avoid this, but the emotion would flow through both of them as their attraction for one another melded with their religious experiences in song and in worship. Jim knew this was a dangerous combination. It was one that could become imprinted into the mind and form permanent bonding. It happened never the less. Jim should have taken action long ago that would have prevented this from unfolding. He had tried, but probably not hard enough. Jim began to notice people watching them. They were watching him in particular. Anyone with evolutionary views about life must be Satanic to some religious people anyway he thought. Jim got particularly hard looks from the Minister of Music on Wednesday night, some even by the Preacher. Their non verbal first glance was like "Uh Oh, he's here again." Like they thought Jim had come just to "court" this married lady. This was not Jim's intent, although something of this nature appeared to be happening. Once in the morning service at church, the minister of music, having led the choir in song, returned to sit in the choir itself after the sermon had begun, something very unusual. Not only that, he sat right behind Angela in a direct line with Jim and scowled at him as Jim looked toward Angela. Jim was not sure if Angela was privy to what was going on. Her husband was walking up the outside isle as the minister of music was doing this. There she was in the center of three men's attention, the minister of music scowling at Jim, Jim looking at Angela, and her husband's presence very obvious to everyone. Jim thought the minister of music had staged this. He noticed Angela became very uneasy, so he thought she didn't know this was going to happen. Jim looked away and diverted his attention elsewhere. He wondered if the minister of music thought he was trying to mesmerize Angela with some kind of satanic power, and he was trying to intervene. Jim couldn't believe that Angela had anything to do with this, but it was a possibility. At first she may have complained, but it was nothing she couldn't have resolved in the very beginning by being open and speaking to Jim about it, but she never would. One would think that a simple conversation between the two of them could have solved this communication problem, but they would both become almost speechless when an opportunity of this nature presented itself. She would not allow Jim the chance to talk this thing out when they were around anyone who could witness the discussion. Jim's love for her father and mother had prevented him from approaching the officers of the Church or anyone else lest he implicate their daughter in a Church scandal.

Satan was mentioned more and more in the Sunday messages as the cause of many difficulties, and questions like, "Why do bad things happen to good people?", were discussed. Of course this could have been coincidence but it sure didn't seem like it to Jim. When the statement, "He is not hers and she is not his." was thrown out in an emotion filled passage, it just clenched it for

Jim. The preacher was talking about Angela and him. Members were becoming concerned he thought. It seemed that the preacher was trying to solve this difficult problem "innocuously" through sermons and teaching. He certainly was not talking to Jim personally about anything, or was anyone else. Jim knew one's imagination could be a factor in high stress situations such as these. One thing he knew for sure though; they had experienced an emotional and spiritual bond. It was obvious to Jim. Without verbal communication of feelings and intent, Jim did not know for sure how she felt. Jim knew his attraction for her was on the highest level of behavior and anticipation on his part. He had no thought of breaking this lady's marriage.

The New Year was beginning, and many visionary goals were being set for the church. Jim feared the leaders might expect "Satin" to try to disrupt their work. The work of "Satin" had been in open discussion at times. He thought his relationship with Angela might be just right to blame for any failures. Jim was at work at the hospital one Sunday night at a time when the church leaders would normally be in a session of prayer. He visited the hospital Chapel and wrote a prayer of supplication and sent it to the Pastor. The pastor did not talk to Jim about it directly, but the general mood of the leaders improved. The pastor had not talked personally to Jim about any of this. Jim believed Angela had read the prayer, judging from comments made by the pastor in a service that only Jim would be able to connect to this writing. He could not be sure, but Jim thought she was communicating with the pastor about this situation. To Jim, many people were aware of their attraction for each other. She couldn't stop looking amorously at Jim regardless of what objections she may have had in the beginning. In the services it was very obvious, particularly when the songs were being sung. Jim would sing out, and she would respond emotionally to his singing. Jim would accentuate the various phrases in the hymns with emotion and feeling, as he had always done. He communicated a sense of love and caring, of man and the spirit that was real inside of him. Her response was always positive it seemed, with reciprocal feelings of spirituality expressed with strong emotion. She never tried to reject any of their emotional contact.

Often, when Jim sat reading in the sanctuary prior to the Wednesday night service, she would come in from a doorway in the front of the church and walk down the side isle where he sat. They always greeted each other. Jim would say, "Hi, how are you?" or something similar, and she would return the greeting. A lot of unspoken emotion transpired between them, however. She would walk on by; go out the back door of the sanctuary and into the vestibule where the library was located. Jim always had the feeling she wanted him to follow her back there to meet. He really wanted to do so. Jim really wanted to express his personal feelings, and also to clear the air of any possibility of a real amorous relationship. He would not, however, and never did because he was not sure of her intentions. Entrapment, Jim felt, though hard to swallow, was a possibility. Later on one Wednesday night, she came by. They greeted like they always had, but when she turned away she was blushed with emotion and began to cry. This really upset Jim. Jim thought to himself, "Was she weeping for me or for what might happen to me? Was she being put up to do this?" When enough people had entered the vestibule for the service to preclude any intent on Jim's part, he went out to see. As he passed out the door into the vestibule, her husband passed by. He had a camera on a strap over his shoulder. He looked startled when he saw Jim.

These kinds of experiences led Jim to believe that he knew, as well as others, about their involvement and was trying to establish factual information to support his claim. She may have told them Jim was enticing (coming on to) her. Her husband might have been trying to capture her in a compromising situation. Jim could never really sort this out, however, because of other experiences. Once in church during the service, they were looking at each other as the message was preached. Jim was seated on the pew next to Dorothy. Dorothy moved right up close to him and began touching and looking at him with affection. At that very moment, Angela got up and walked out of the choir and out of the sanctuary right in the middle of the service. Jim thought, "Why did she do this?" "Was she objecting because she thought he had fallen for her and thought he was hers? Or was she objecting because Dorothy was insinuating that she had an interest in her husband?" Kind of like Dorothy was saying to her, "He's mine, stop staring at him and stay away from him."

In another incident, right at the end of a service at the altar call, Jim had to go to the bathroom and could not wait. Angela and Jim had been glancing at each other in this emotional part of the service. Jim left. He had to. When he came back she was standing there weeping, the tears running down her cheeks. Jim almost broke up. He questioned again to himself, "Had she been praying for him, even for his own salvation maybe, and he had walked out? Did she think he had walked out on her amorous attention? Jim didn't know. Mixed signals and no real communication of intents had Jim confused.

Jim decided to write the pastor and her dad a letter. In the letter Jim mentioned that he was not making excuses for his feelings, but many people did not really know him and could well have misunderstandings about what they thought was happening. Jim indicated outright he was not a promiscuous person and had not been unfaithful to his wives. He apologized for actually having "wives" this had never been his desire. He explained how negative feelings could have come from his position concerning science and the faith and from gossip and misunderstandings that had followed him from his teaching position when he retired. Jim never received any comments from the preacher or her dad about what he had communicated in the letter. They never acknowledged they had received any information from him.

Jim rehashed some of the things that might have influenced T. W. and others to have the questionable opinion of him they seemed to be projecting. Jim thought her dad may have had wind of some of his activities because his son was a school board member and was privy to comments made by other school leaders.

One of T. W.'s Sunday school class members had died soon after Jim's attendance in that class began, and the class was to serve as active and inactive pallbearers. Jim noticed T. W. was uncomfortable with his presence and made sure he was not an active pallbearer. Jim wondered if T. W. had heard some of the gossip about his activities with Betsy and Roy and maybe even about some of his relations with Dorothy, his wife, through one of his high school principals and his friends. Before Jim married Dorothy, an employee and relative of workers for the school board had seen his car at Dorothy's house on the Bayview Highway one morning and "admonished" him about it saying, "I never thought you were that kind of person." Jim knew that Dorothy had a previous "boyfriend" that was in Viet Nam. He didn't know at the time her boyfriend was the son of a Lakeshore County Principal and also relative to many in the school system. One of Jim's students at Pine Ridge High School had dated Dorothy. Jim could guess what might have transpired behind the scenes from this. One day following the comment made about him by the school worker, Jim was addressed by one of the County School Board Officers very rudely, suggesting promiscuous activity. He was related to the worker who had criticized him. Jim reprimanded him, and told him that his name was Jim Josephson and that was how he should address him. Jim's principal when he retired, not his principal friend that had first hired him, had knowledge of some of this. He was always good to Jim and Jim liked him, but he would not promote Jim's leadership ability or give him any leadership role. He ostracized him from the "in" group that Jim enjoyed at Pine Ridge. Jim thought the general idea that he was a "ladies" man was communicated to female members of the faculty. Some members of that school faculty are members of Lakeview Baptist Church. Later, speaking by innuendo in a conversation concerning these impressions, Angela's father had said to Jim, "I think they are just jealous." Jim had pondered this remark T. W. had made at the time. He remembered a comment a student friend made to him shortly before he retired from teaching. The young man was a member of a local church going family. They attended a small church in the school community. He had said, "Mr. Josephson, we hear you've got yourself a new girlfriend." Jim replied, "What do you mean? I am married. I don't need a new girlfriend." "That's not what we are hearing." He said. "Everybody knows you are a "stud" Mr. Josephson." Embarrassed, Jim knew he had never needed an athletic trophy to establish his physical prowess. He remembered the "look" Angela had given him at her father's home.

Chapter Ten

Jim was feeling the emotional strain of all of this and apparently the unspoken desire by some, including Angela, for him to come down to alter call and confess whatever they thought he was guilty of, when his cousin who lived in Fort Walton died.

Jim traveled over in his truck to the funeral, and on his way he missed the turn off road. Jim was approaching a bridge to Bay View Island. To avoid delay he made an unlawful left turn into a roadway. A deputy in a county car saw him make the turn. A short distance down the road the deputy stopped him. Jim explained what had happened. The Officer instructed Jim to wait until he returned from his car. When he returned, he walked up to the window of Jim's truck where he was sitting and said, "It would be wrong to give you a ticket today, Mr. Josephson. You go on to the funeral. Here is how you can get to the church." The comment, "It would be wrong to give you a ticket", startled Jim and made him think. Jim had been stopped many times in his life for traffic violations and never had one of the officers said it would be wrong to cite him. Jim took it as a spiritual message of exoneration because he was filled with deep feelings of remorse.

The service was beautiful, and Jim was filled with emotion. Jim wrote a creative piece about this experience. Later he gave this piece to her dad, his Sunday school teacher. T. W. read it in the Sunday school class to the men. He seemed upbeat and commented that one never lost opportunities to make contributions to the work of the Lord. Jim really thought he expected him to make repentance at the altar for his "advances" toward his daughter. He thought he had read this in the line, "Just go on forward and be bold." but

Jim was referring to life in general, not about going forward to the altar. Jim had never made any intentional "advances" toward his daughter. What had happened between them was spontaneous and mutual and she was responsible, for her own actions toward him. Jim didn't need to go there and confess this to his silent accusers. Jim had already confessed his emotional relationship to T. W. and others. He could see at the end of the next morning service that Angela was disappointed. She looked over at her dad as she left the choir with a, "I thought you told me he was going to do this" look. The very next Sunday the minister of music sang the very same song that that was so moving to Jim at the funeral. The rendition of the song was the motivating incident for the creative work. The colored man who sang it at the funeral was better. Was it a coincidence? Jim thought. Not to him. They knew and were involved and communicating in this situation but none were talking directly to him about any of it for some reason. Jim's point of view seemed irrelevant to them. He really couldn't understand this because when he and Angela met she was more engaged and involved in her emotional relationship with him than he was with her. All that was missing to rectify this situation was communication between Jim and Angela in a Christian manner. Somehow, communication between them could never be accomplished. Friends tried. Jim knew some had tried to help them breach this impasse. She would never open up to him or allow him to talk to her about this situation. Jim tried, but she avoided every attempt on his part.

As events unfolded, Jim noticed her mother and dad were beginning to give him a lot of attention. They sat with him at the Wednesday night supper while their daughter and Jim unavoidably made eye contact. Husband had disappeared at this point. Jim didn't know where he was, but he wasn't with her at the suppers. Mom and dad almost always sat with him or near him in the prayer service. The minister of music had long since stopped leading singing at the opening and none of the young couples that formally sat in front of him attended. Their daughter did not attend much during this time. One bothersome observation was Angela's apparent lack of a strong relationship with her daughters. Jim seldom saw her with them.

Jim was sitting with T. W. one night at a Wednesday night supper. Jackie, her mother, was not there. Dorothy had given him a new diamond ring for their wedding anniversary, and Jim was wearing it on his right hand. T. W. approached the other side of Jim's table across from him and they began to talk. "Well, come on and sit down, T. W. We have some good food tonight, don't we?" "Yeah, we sure do." T. W. said, "I told Jackie she should have come tonight. This ham is really delicious." "I know, I've eaten two pieces already." Jim said. "How is everyone in your family, T. W.?" "Jackie has been having those old headaches again. That's why she is not here." He noticed Jim looking up at Angela who was about to sit down at a table in the middle section of seats. "Angela has those things, too." He said, as if to indicate he had seen Jim look up at her. "Yes. I know" Jim said. "It must be difficult for both of them." Angela had turned to look at Jim again after she sat down. T. W. was watching. As if to break the attention she was giving Jim, he said, "What have you been doing lately, Jim? Have you been working at the hospital?" "I work Thursdays, Fridays and weekends. I haven't worked any the first of this week." "What do you do with all that time off? I know you are an active person." "I do a lot of local traveling. I go to local historical sites. I just love traveling in the country. Oh, T. W.! Let me tell you what happened the other day." I went up to Troy Alabama to Troy University. I attended Troy when it was Troy State College. I saw a building named the Sorrell building. The Pathologist at the lab school I attended was named Walker B. Sorrell. I wanted to find out if it was named after him. I went to an administrative building and walked into the vestibule. I asked the attendant at the desk about the building. She said she was sorry she didn't know the answer. I should go down the hall on the right and they could tell me all I needed to know. A pretty young lady going by down the hall had noticed us and heard her say this. The attendant then said, "Just follow that lady there. She is going there." I started off behind the lady down the hall. In just a second, I realized where she was going. I said. "You are going to the women's restroom aren't you?" "Yes, I am." She laughed. "I'm not going in there to try to find out anything!" I laughed. "Just go on down to the next door, that's the one she meant." She said laughingly. I walked on down and through the door to the desk. A young college student was at the desk. I asked her about the Sorrell building. She didn't know either and said that the person in the office was out to lunch. He would be back in shortly. I had talked to her for about five minutes when a well dressed man and a lady walked through the door. They greeted me as they passed, and I returned the greeting. I stepped forward toward them and said, "Pardon me sir, but can I ask you a question?" The man turned to me and said. "Sure. What do you want to know?" "The Sorrell building across the way over there, is it named for Walker B. Sorrell who was the Pathologist at St. Margaret's Hospital in Montgomery?" "No." He said. "It was named after a business man in the lumber business who has contributed greatly to this University. I know who you are talking about, but no, it was not named for him." We carried on a lively conversation about the University. I indicated that I was an alumnus, and we talked about that. He even went to his office and got a Troy University T shirt and gave it to me. He suggested I visit the Alumni building close by before I left. I said I would. As we gave parting comments, I said: "By the way, I am Jim Josephson, what is your name?" He said, "I am Bob Riley, and it has been a real pleasure talking with you today, Mr. Josephson." I said, "It has been a pleasure for me too, Mr. Riley." I turned and left the office. I went by the Alumni building and then on toward home. Down the road between Opp and Florala, Alabama, I stopped at a rest station. No one was there but me. I walked through the door and saw a picture of a man on the wall in front of me. As I neared, I could tell he looked familiar. Even closer, I exclaimed outloud, "That's the man I just talked to!" The man at the desk looked around at me. I read the caption under the picture, "Governor Bob Riley" "That's the Governor of Alabama!" I blurted out. I turned to the man at the desk in excitement. "I just talked to the Governor of Alabama and didn't know it! The security officer said, "Well, he's just a man like anybody else." "But he was the *Governor*!" I said.

After Jim finished, they were laughing and talking at the table about the story Jim had just told. Jim put his hand down on the table right in front of T. W. He noticed him look down at the new ring on his right hand. He knew it was a new ring when he saw it. He became filled with emotion. Tears began to flood into his eyes, and he had to turn his head away to keep from breaking up. Jim was distraught. He wondered why the ring had caused him to react the way he did with so much emotion. Did he think Angela had given him this ring? Did he have some knowledge of her intentions toward Jim and the deep emotional involvement she had with him? Did he realize then what Angela was facing? How could Jim know when no one would communicate to him, not even Angela?

One night as Jim was coming to prayer meeting in his truck, He passed Angela and one of her girl friends going the other way. Jim knew they saw him, and he said to himself, "That was Angela and Cathy." She drove a blue Ford Aerostar with a missing right front hub cap. Jim went on to the service, and before the service started Angela and Cathy came in and sat down. Angela was dressed differently and had on a red shade of lipstick, something Jim had never seen her wear. She usually attended choir practice after the service. As Jim left the prayer meeting, He looked back through the church and there stood Angela, looking at him and posturing in such a way as to say, "I'm available." Her eyes were sparking with his and to him it was an invitation. He really felt a powerful urge to go and embrace her. Being the man Jim was, He couldn't help but want to, all of these years of emotion and attraction, but he could not. This was when Jim really began to worry. Did she just want sexual attention, or was she so serious she was willing to leave her husband? Jim was fearful of this because he knew how he felt about commitment and marriage, and besides, this had happened to him. She began to appear more often, prior to the prayer meeting. Once she came to talk to one of the pianists who was sitting in front of Jim waiting for the service to begin. This lady was also one of the supervisors for the school system and had been recently divorced. As she talked to her, she continuously looked passed her at Jim, obviously so, with this air of freedom and release and seemed to say to him, "I am available." Jim had strong feelings of emotion. He knew how much he was attracted to her now, how much their lives were spiritually connected, but Jim knew he could not do anything like that. Rationally this was the wrong thing to do. He had never wanted this relationship to proceed in this manner. This was very distressing. Jim had to do *something*.

The next time Jim walked into her dad's Sunday school class, he said outright to him. "I have got to talk to you." He probably should have just forced a conversation with Angela, but the opportunity would always elude him and besides he wasn't sure of her intentions. In the meantime Jim sent T. W. an e-mail. He spoke in metaphor about something he was sure T. W. already understood. Jim said he thought all of this was of God and not Satan. Jim asked for his help as a Christian to solve this problem even though he had not been direct and specific. Jim said he thought T. W. knew what he was talking about and that if he didn't he was really confused. Jim mentioned he loved them. He offered to keep everything discussed between them confidential.

T. W. never answered this e-mail. As a matter of fact, he never answered any e-mail and finally had Jim blocked. Eventually, after several verbal requests on Jim's part, dad came to Jim's house to see him. They visited cordially, and he looked at Jim's home, buildings and garden. T. W. was impressed. As they talked on the porch, Jim found the courage to approach him about matters Jim thought, he already knew. Jim explained to him he had an attraction for Angela. Jim withheld any criticism of Angela or any discussion of her involvement. T. W. appeared shocked. He said he knew nothing about any of this and was not aware of anything like this. He said he was "clueless" as to what Jim's letter had meant. He said Angela and her husband were fine. Jim asked him if Angela was angry with him. He replied very emphatically and with a caring smile, "Oh no, no. Angela is not angry with you." Jim finally asked him outright if he thought what was happening was just a one way thing on his part, if it was just him. T. W. said, "Yes. I think it is. I think it is just you." Jim told him he always thought otherwise, but he could be wrong. T. W. said, "Let's not tell her mother anything like that."

Jim said, "Oh no, we don't need to tell mother anything." After a little more discussion, and when T. W. was off guard a little, Jim asked, "What happened to us, T. W.?" He said, "It just happened. It just happened." Without realizing it at first, T. W. had told Jim he knew that his daughter was personally involved. Then he began to disclose strange things to Jim. He related in confidence about some of his own personal experiences. He explained about his older son's divorce, how he went before the church and confessed his adultery; how he had divorced and remarried; how great everything was going. Jim told him he made that sound so good, so as to make it all right. T. W. said, "No, it was not all right." Jim replied, "I'm glad you said that." For the most part, that ended their conversation about Angela.

Jim had ignored what he *thought* were Angela's advances, and he noticed some indications that her husband was reappearing. As good as this was, Jim knew it would not end it. One Wednesday night Angela was serving in the kitchen for the guests. It was a church benefit dinner for a group of girls. Jim was afraid of what might happen. When he reached her station in the serving line, He looked down at the large ring on her finger, and then he looked up at her. Jim knew better, but he could not stop looking at her hair, her neck and face, and then the eyes. When their eyes met, they locked in a deep emotional compassion. Her eyes never wavered, never blinked, never turned away. Jim was flooded with emotion. As he turned to leave, Jim looked back and said to her, "Angela, are you ok?" She said, "Yes I'm fine, are **you** ok?" I said, "Yes I'm ok, I'm ok," in a regretful tone.—Jim knew *he* wasn't ok. He took his dinner over to the table to eat. When he looked over where Angela was, she was staring at him with this forlorn look on her face as if she was in deep spiritual agony, in a deep emotional need. Jim was heartbroken. Jim realized then what a deep conundrum he was in. His marriage compromised, even though nothing had happened, and he still loved Dorothy and the boys. Jim was really in emotional and spiritual agony. Later that night he had a remarkable experience. He wrote an account and sent it to her dad, accompanied with the following letter. That's all he knew to do.

Reflections to Loved Ones

Whether behavior is rational or irrational is often in the eyes of the beholder. Consider for instance this scripture. I have thought over this passage since I was a child. "But whereunto shall I liken this generation? It is like unto children sitting in the markets and calling unto their fellows, and saying, "We have piped unto you and ye have not danced; we have mourned unto you, and ye have not lamented. For John came neither eating nor drinking, and they say, He hath a devil. The Son of man came eating and drinking, and they say, Behold a man gluttonous, and a wine bibber, a friend of publicans and sinners."[1] We all try to justify our own inconsistencies as we pass our judgments on others. What think ye of me; Rational? Irrational? An instrument of God? An instrument of the devil? These are tough questions for one to have to face. Through history men have been crucified and burned at the stake just for their different views, each party swearing to God and standing behind their interpretations of scripture. And yes, they were ultimately judged by each other, probably not by God, on this earth at least. And probably, if someone should ask outright: "Do you love this person?" I would say yes, but also like Christ loved and with no selfish intentions. "Do you hate this person?" I would say no. It is very hard for me to hate. What credibility would you give my view if I said it came from God? These are hard questions to answer while onlookers gawk, as it is played out in real life and real lives. I can here Christ's on claim to scripture; "They point the finger, they mock", and all the while, his heart was filled with the love of God, but they made him to appear as a blasphemer, punishable with death, and this was his agony and his Passion.

---

[1]   Matthew 11:16-19.(KJV)

So conflicting views, unresolved heartaches, deep misunderstandings, and unknown intentions, bring stress to bear on the emotional aspects of our lives, but Christ is there in our hearts and in despair we reach out to Him; we pour out our hearts to Him and He helps us understand because He has been there. He lifts us and gives us peace.

Whether I am rational or irrational in your eyes, I want to share with you this experience. I pray you will keep it in your hearts and know that I did not intentionally ever want to hurt or become a stumbling block for anyone. I just ask for your forgiveness where I might have hurt or failed anyone. I just give to you my heart and ask Christ to do with it as His will sees fit.

Love to you all,

Jim.

The experience Jim spoke of had been a dream. When Jim retired that night, after the encounter with Angela at the serving line, he realized how emotionally distressed he was over this situation. When he prayed Jim asked the Lord for help in this difficult time. Jim said the Lord knew he had prayed so much and so many times for others, but now he must pray for himself. With these thoughts on his mind Jim went to sleep and began to dream. Jim dreamed he was in Church on a Wednesday night and the service was beginning to close. Jim began to search through the Church until he found this closet. He went into the closet and knelt on the floor. Jim began to pray. As he began to pray he began to weep and could not stop weeping. Someone who was closing the Church heard him and called out: "Who is in there?" He said: "It's Jim." Eventually Jim opened the door and it was Phillip Thomas a good friend of his. Phil asked: "What are you doing in here?" And Jim said: "Well the Bible says to go into your closet and pray." At that, Phil came inside the closet and began to pray with Jim. Jim awoke the next morning with full memory of this dream and also with tremendous emotional release and ease in his heart, and Jim knew his prayer was answered by this dream.

The next Wednesday night Angela was at dinner alone. Dad, mother and Jim were sitting together. After most everyone had finished and left, Angela got up from her seat, and came straight toward Jim and her dad. She was looking right at Jim with a look of resolution. She sat down in front of Jim beside her dad, leaned over and kissed her dad amorously on the cheek. She said, "Thank you dad, It looks like I am going to have to come over and live with you, the noise and everything—" Jim suffers from hearing loss, and he could not make out the rest of what she said. He did hear her say, "I could just hug his neck." To which her dad replied, "No, no, don't do that." Jim had said in the letter that whatever they were experiencing was of God. Jim thought this was the key. He really believed in his heart she had read this letter. He had always believed that Angela had experienced some kind of spiritual revelation that had promoted her to react the way she had toward him. Jim left without saying anything more, just parting comments. Jim was moved by this but he was deeply worried. He knew he had not made any commitments like he "thought" she was anticipating.

After this encounter, Jim took a ride in the country. Jim usually goes to the old places where he, his dad, and Uncle Oliver had such great times together to reminisce. He takes hold again to those values and expectations that these great men in his life placed in him. He sometimes goes to the towns and hamlets where he and his uncle did business and made friends. While he is enjoying the scenery, the memories, He searches the heart and seeks the Spirit.

He left Lakeshore and intersected old highway One Ninety One toward Munson, Florida, took the Belandville road, crossed over to the Beaver Creek road and out to Alabama State Highway Four. He took Highway Four west across the Conecuh River to U. S. Highway Twenty Nine. He turned to the right going north on Twenty Nine. He knew of a road intersecting highway Twenty Nine from the north that went to a small hamlet called Damascus. He thought to himself, "If Paul could meet Jesus on the road to Damascus, maybe I can." As he drove out this road toward Damascus, he began to ruminate over everything that had happened between him and Angela. He poured out his heart over the events that had taken place. He went down every avenue of consideration, every tidbit of knowledge, trying to understand what had happened and why. He knew that none of this had ever been intentional on his part. With great grief and remorse, Jim came away from this introspection knowing he could not do anything that would hurt his Christian Brother even if Angela gave him the opportunity. He could not allow this to continue and break the promises he had made to his wife and family and to Jesus. He could not do this to this beautiful lady and beautiful children even if she wanted him to. Jim's heart was filled with grief, much grief, over what had unfolded, and he went away with sorrow in his heart, wondering what he had done to his wife, his boys, her husband, and what they had done to themselves.

After Wednesday night supper was over the next Wednesday night, her dad and a gentleman were watching Angela and Jim still exchanging glances as always. They were making joking comments about it, though somewhat disguised. Her dad said, "I don't mind being a go between for them." When most everyone had left, including the gentleman to whom he was talking, Jim related to her dad what had happened to him; "When I was about thirty, this rich man came into my wife's life and took my wife and children away from me. I know the difficulty and suffering involved in all of this. I could never do that to anyone, I don't think. I just couldn't do it. "No, no," he said, "You couldn't do that." Jim also reminded him that in two years he would be seventy years old. He related that Angela's birthday is about the same as his own daughter's birthday. Then Jim commented, "You can't take another man's wife from him unless she wants to leave to begin with." Jim certainly was not trying to take anyone, but unfortunately, he knew something about it. It seemed to him she was pressuring him to leave his wife. T. W. never said anything about these comments. They parted company and went into the sanctuary.

Jim sent the preacher this letter after this soul searching, heart wrenching, trip with the spirit of Jesus at Damascus.

October 4, 2006
1406 South Court Street
Lakeshore Florida 32570

The Reverend Steve Faircloth
Lakeview Church
Lakeshore, FL 32570

Dear Reverend Faircloth:

I want to thank you for messages on Christian relationships and problem solving. I do not think I have met anyone who reflects my feeling more about what the bible says about spiritual relationships, and the meaning of real Christianity in the here and now. I know I differ in some details of interpretation and world view, but your love of Christ is so obvious. Your understanding of love is so deep and sincere. I know you have experienced the essence of real Christian love. How can I know this? Well it's like the bible says, we love Him because He first loved us "unconditionally". And I love you Brother Steve.

Never have I had a time in my life when I struggled harder with two of the aspects of our spiritual selves, reason and emotion. We know that a blend of both is healthy and the best. But we know that in some experiences, we must rely on reason alone to guide us. I remember quite clearly you saying, "God does not call us to do something wrong." I have relied on this, but I have to admit, with great difficulty and struggle, because there is an element of the will of God in all of this that I can know only from my perspective, for no one will confide in me. Never have I been faced with such impossible circumstances. I know my sins, we all do, and the Lord knows I have confessed them and asked for forgiveness from Him first and from others.

But I also know my heart and the spirit of Christ tries hard to live there.

I have included a creative writing, "The resurrection of the Soul". The second paragraph is a bit dramatic. I know of no one who has actually said that or thought that in their heart. It is an imagination of my own that is never the less real in difficult struggles such as these. I know I have thought many times, "If they just knew my heart", not that it would exonerate me but give an entirely different perspective. Well I think that all of this has something to do with that.

It would not be appropriate to express the deep personal feelings of my heart in all of this, but their hopes were clear and pure and beautiful for everyone concerned, as clear and beautiful as the sky on a sunny day over Taylorville and Farmville, Alabama.

Sincerely yours,

Jim Josephson

The Resurrection of the Soul

Once the light of heaven, which radiates from the soul, reflected itself off the magnificent beauty of a holy sanctuary. From the cross to the lofted ceiling, it resonated with the vision and hopes of spiritual visionaries of old. In communion with the souls of spiritual seekers all around, the holy songs from the yearning minds of old lifted the heart to spiritual highs not experienced in the realm of selfish desire and selfish intent. But this longing of the heart was not known by all, some questioned and mistrusted the intentions of its presence there.

"We know you! They cried secretly in their hearts." "The sinful son of the world and that is your home, perverting the worship with sensual desires and selfish intentions."

"Oh no!" some cried openly, "We are all sinful sons of the world, we must cast off our desires and become one with the spirit of love and understanding." "Yes, it is sinful desire that corrupts the heart, but who can know the desire of the heart, without knowing the one who possesses it?" "Who can know it without seeing the outpouring of his soul?" "And yes, who has not experienced it himself?" "And besides, He is not hers and she is not his."

Worship dimmed to the flickering of a flame as the suffering soul searched himself for evidence of their claim. And yes, it was there and yet it wasn't. Out of the purity of a searching heart and yearning spirit, a forbidden desire was looming. But no, this was not the driving force of the soul. This was not the promise by the enlightening spirit that had visited him. What it promised was holy in every way. What it promised was a road to righteousness, not vain hope in evil desire. Surely it was a purging of the soul by the act of an angel, and he knew this angel. What grief fell upon him for himself, for his church, for his witness, for Christ, and for the angel sent from God.

"Oh my soul, I am dying with grief!" "No, my son, you are not dying with grief. Grief is purging your soul as with hyssop and lifting you to a new spiritual enlightenment. You are dying to the selfish desires that force men's hearts to fail, and I am dying with you or I have not died at all. "Then hold my hand." "Yes! I will hold your hand, but not to death but to the resurrection of righteous desire and holy heart that you yearned for in the beginning. I am in you and you are in me, and she is in me, and I and the Father are one. Together we will go and meet Him on this earth in the hearts of His children, and they will know Me, and I will know them and they will see you with me, and know you and they will embrace us." "Take not only my hand but the essence of my being." "Oh my son, I Am the essence of your being, and we shall dwell together in My Father's house forever."

Pastor Faircloth knew quite well what Jim was alluding to in this creative writing. The quote, "He is not hers and she is not his." was his quote from part of one of his emotion-filled sermons which basically iterated the paragraph above that contains this quote. The reference to children was a reference to Jesus' church, his disciples. The reference was not intentionally referring to Angela's children when it was written. Jim never received any acknowledgment of, or comments about, this letter or this writing from the preacher or anyone. Jim was left to stand alone. He realized that if she really did expect some kind of action on his part when she went to her dad's, He needed to communicate with someone. Jim wrote her dad this letter.

Dear T. W., Jacquelyn and family.

I know you must tire of this one-way disclosure, but this is everyone else's choice not mine. I am blind, like Lee at Gettysburg, except for what the Lord would allow me to see. The things I disclosed to you, asked of you, and promised to you and your family are genuine and true, but I must remind you of my belief in the sanctity of marriage and my commitment to my family. Some things in this are larger than life, and only the Lord knows its purpose.

Love always, (I pray earnestly)

Jim

During this time, Dorothy had scheduled a hysterectomy to be performed at a local hospital. T. W. and Jacqueline came to visit them there and they waited for five hours for the surgery to be completed. Angela's dad seemed to be consumed with emotion. When Dorothy's mother entered the waiting room, he had to hide behind a newspaper to keep from showing his emotion. He was at the point of tears. Jim really wondered why he was like this and later Jim asked Denise (his mother-in-law) if she knew him. She said she had never seen him before. The preacher was there, and he and T. W. started talking about Angela's husband, Mark. On and on they went about his good relationship with Angela and the things he could do. After a while, Jim couldn't take any more, so he got up and walked out. T. W. followed him out and into the bathroom. They talked, but not about anything related to Angela. Everything was a mystery to Jim. Why all of the emotion? Why all of the talk? Eventually the surgeon came out to inform them of the outcome. When Jim saw her (she is a female gynecologist) he was greatly relieved, and she quickly assured him that Dorothy was ok. Jim embraced her as he thanked her. Angela's Mom and dad stood up to say goodbye. They had been there for five hours. Jim embraced them and told them he loved them. As Angela's mother was leaving, she said to him. "You just go on with your little wife, that's what you need to do." Why did she say this to him? This led Jim to believe that Angela's mother knew about Angela's intentions toward him. Angela had never talked to Jim about any of her intentions. Jim was ignorant about what she must have thought he knew or intended to do. Jim really wondered about all of this. In one of his writings, he had told them that things would work out in such a way as to not hurt anyone. By that, Jim meant in a Christian manner. Jim wondered if their curious behavior had anything to do with this comment. He thought to himself, "Were they looking for something to happen to my wife? God forbid. Surely my imagination is running away with me."

Angela did leave her home. She took her children and went to her dad's home. Her dad made a comment in their Sunday school class that she was there. He said her husband was remodeling their house. He explained that the noise and dust was too much for them, and she needed to move while that part was finished. This could have been absolutely true as far as Jim knew, but he doubted that as the underlying reason. Jim never tried to precipitate anything. He stayed at home. He didn't go anywhere near dad's house, but it was a heartbreaking experience. Jim didn't want to hurt her. One day while she was at dads, Joseph and Jim went to Arby's to get something to eat. They were sitting at a table talking and in came some people Jim didn't know. They had several children with them. Jim looked over at the tables where they were sitting and one of Angela's daughters was sitting there with them. When she saw Jim her face flushed, she started to cry, got up and went into the bathroom, and did not come out. Jim was flabbergasted. Why did this child do this? He had never really met her and had never spoken to her that he could remember. Jim knew then something that involved him and her children had happened in Angela's family. He wondered what it possibly could have been.

At a Wednesday dinner one night while Angela was staying with her father, Jim was standing in the serving line with T. W. They began to converse with one other. He was getting take out dinners, and Angela was not there. He said he was taking the dinners home because they weren't feeling well. Jim knew Angela had a history of migraines so he commented. "It's not Angela is it, One of the migraines?" He said, "Yes, Angela wasn't feeling well and wouldn't be coming." Jim sat down to eat after being served and in about ten minutes Angela bolted into the room, went to the serving line and got a dinner. As she turned to go to the table in the back where she usually sat with friends, her husband came in and followed her to the table. There was an air of defiance about Angela in this, and Jim wondered why her dad had said what he did. He wondered if, perchance, they were trying to keep Angela from seeing him. Angela attended prayer meeting that night but not with her husband. She was with some of her girl friends. She made no effort to talk with Jim. He could never understand why she would never speak to him about her interest which she had made too obvious to be misunderstood.

Eventually Angela went back home. Jim supposed when the work was complete, although her husband was still working on the house. Jim noticed that her activity was beginning to move into places that he frequented. She began parking right where Jim parked his truck. He met her casually several times in the vestibule when normally he wouldn't. It was as if she was trying to make contact with him. Once she was with a friend and had her youngest daughter with her. It was one of the very few times he had ever seen her with one of her children. It looked as if she had come there to talk to him with her child, but an older member of the church kept detaining him (seemingly to him, on purpose), and they did not meet. Then one Sunday at the morning service, something really puzzling occurred. Dorothy and Jim had decided to sit up toward the middle of the church that Sunday. Normally, they sat in the back right corner. Sometime Jim sat there alone when Dorothy had nursery duty. After the service was over, Dorothy and Jim were standing at the end of the pew where they had been seated. Jim looked around and Angela was coming out of the corner they usually sat in. She was dressed in a pretty print dress; the first one Jim had ever seen her wear. She was leading the same child as before, her youngest daughter, by the hand. When she looked over and saw Jim and Dorothy together, she began to cry and turned her face away from him. Jim was broken. He was moved with deep grief and emotion. He did not know her intent, but he knew whatever it was was very important to her. "Could it possibly have involved her child?" He thought. She seemed to be bringing her child to him to talk or something.

Jim went to see her dad at his home after this. He did this because he loved him and his family so much. Jim was trying so hard to avert any hurt or hard feelings. Jim avoided any conversation about Angela for a while, but they finally got around to it. "How is Angela doing these days T. W.? I have been really concerned about her lately. Did you receive the letter I sent you?" T. W. commented. "I am clueless about what any of your writings mean and am really confused about your behavior. Angela and Mark are doing just fine. Jim replied. "I really can't understand that T. W. after everything that's unfolded. How could you not understand what they were about? Do you think she would quit the choir if I tried to join?" "You are asking the wrong person. You will need to ask her about that. Really, what makes you think Angela has any interest in you anyway?" T. W. asked. "Well T. W. I just know things you can't know. Angela just needs to stay with her husband and be happy. What was made in heaven will just have to stay in heaven." Jim just couldn't discuss any more of this with him. He just couldn't question or criticize his daughter in front of him. Jim just loved him too much.

After this meeting, Jim sent this letter to the preacher, Brother Steve. The first comments concern a story about a hunting experience that Jim included with the letter.

October 23, 2006
1406 South Court Street
Lakeshore Florida 32570

Reverend Steve Faircloth D.D.
8550 County Line Drive
Lakeshore, FL 32570

Dear Dr. Faircloth:

I thought I would share this true story about a family
place name with you. You will need to excuse an expletive
and a few other descriptive terms, (I know you will not
like them), but they needed to be there because it actually
happened somewhat like that. I have had many experiences
in my life. The first twenty years or so of companionship
was experience almost entirely with mature adult men
who were my relatives. I could not have asked for a more
wholesome environment. My father and special uncle
were my role models. My mother and her sister married
my dad and his brother. They lived next door to us. My
uncle was sterile and could not have children. My sister
and I in effect had two sets of parents. The sisters were
devout Presbyterian Christians and attended church and
participated in most of its activities. Next to Moses, my
father was one of the most humble men I have met in my
life, and yet, he was physically powerful and mentally
strong. He did not go to church much and was not a
member, but I saw Christ in him easily as I struggled to
grasp Christ's teaching on my own. My mother and aunt
were responsible for the religious and biblical teaching of
my youth. And of course, the Presbyterian Church was
a teaching church. I came to see quite quickly, though,
that the formal church was not the only place you could
see the heart of Christ's teaching being really applied. The
teachings of Christ and the teachings and expectations of

these dear relatives and companions have always been my standard for acceptable behavior. I know a man cannot be measured by the attributes of his parents, but they provide the foundation upon which a child builds his own standards and self expectations. I know I have failed them in some ways, but I know I have loved them and this was all that they asked of me. And this is really all that Christ asks of us, that we will love Him, because He knows if we love Him we will try so hard to keep His commandments. And we will weep with grief when we don't. We tell others about Him, primarily through our love for others, by the expectations we have set for our own selves and by communicating the driving force that shapes our lives.

I apologize again for the mistakes I have made. The mistakes, though, were not in wrongful intent or the willful selfish desires of the heart on my part. They were the result of unfortunate consequences beyond either person's immediate control. They were made in resolving the unfolding difficulty at the onset. Instead of using the principles outlined in the purpose driven life for resolving conflicts, the very opposite actions were put into effect. Third parties became involved who would not communicate, some were officers of the church. No one trusted me enough to present the difficulty straight forward for resolution. I offered to do this in the very beginning to a concerned person speaking to me in public by innuendo but was rejected on the premise that I would just blame the other party. I have done all of the disclosing, and I can do no more. I hope you can see that I am not angry nor do I want to place blame on anyone. It is difficult though when leaders cringe at your presence at certain functions as if they knew your intent and the reason for your presence as a fact and really did not want you to be there. Or to question your presence at a funeral when you had known her for many years and had taught her children in Bible School and Sunday School, or to apparently withhold participation in functions of the church because you were a participant, or to obviously interrupt the atmosphere of worship with an intent of their own, or to earnestly expect your confession and disregard their responsibility to disclose their motives for actions concerning this situation. Well, you might say, that was your fault. Well, fault or not, that is not the Christian approach to the resolution of a difficult problem. It demonstrates a complete lack of faith and trust toward a struggling member of the Christian body. I hope you are not offended by the remarks I have made here. I am certainly not talking about you though; I know you have been burdened with it undeservingly. I could explain many ways I can know and understand how and why many things are unfolding the way they are. I could explain how certain people have purposefully misled me and have bent the truth so to speak. But I understand these things and know why they had to be that way. I hope to see a good and healthy resolution, one acceptable to all and to Christ. I need the confidence and trust of others. Someone (the accuser if there is one) must step forward and present to me, face to face the truth of this situation from their perspective. And I don't mean a third party. I will not be offended nor will I betray their confidence. I will wait patiently. I ask you to keep this communication in confidence. I really don't know how much you understand about all of this. Like I said, I am blind like Lee at Gettysburg.

Sincerely yours,

Jim Josephson

Chapter Eleven

J im knew Angela had compromised a part of his heart. She had also caused him to rehash some of the things that had happened to him and Betsy Lee so long ago. This had begun to be a concern for him. He hadn't seen Betsy Lee for thirty two years. One day he was driving west on highway ninety eight out of Lakeshore and was approaching Roy's old Volkswagen shop. He looked over to view the window as he had done for so many years, and it was gone! This startled him so. This feeling of emptiness came over him as if he was losing a special connection to an important part of his life. Jim learned that new owners had removed the old apartment above the shop and replaced it with new metal sheeting. For Jim, when real love is turned on it cannot ever be completely turned off, and it does not compromise one's love for someone else. In the depths of Jim's heart, it is so much more than just selfish physical desire. It even goes beyond the need to be together.

The last time Jim was in Taylorville on one of his trips through the country, he went back down First Street where Betsy Lee's brother lived. He saw that someone was there so he stopped. Jim knocked on the door. A man answered. "Hello" Jim said. "I am Jim Josephson. I'm sorry to bother you, but I wondered if you might happen to know Betsy Lee Taylor. When I knew her, she was a Harding." "Yes," he said, "She is my sister." "I was just trying to find out about her. I haven't seen her for thirty two years. I was very good friends with her at one time back then." He introduced himself as James Taylor and began to tell him about her, how she had been to Europe with her husband. He was so open that Jim wondered if he might have known about him before hand. Jim told him he thought he had seen where her mother died a year or more ago, and also thought Betsy Lee was in California. No, he said, their mother had died just last month and they buried her here in Taylorville. Betsy Lee was here for the funeral. Jim told him about his family, his boys and what they had accomplished. He asked him if she ever had children. He said no, she never had. Jim was saddened for some reason. He loved her so much. At one time he wanted her to be the mother of his children. She never knew that though. James had several Deer trophies mounted on the wall of his den. They conversed for a few minutes about Betsy Lee and their families and their hunting activities. Jim shared some of his interests with him. He realized they had much in common and they became friends quickly. Jim thanked him for sharing everything with him and for being so open and kind to a stranger. He said goodbye and left. Jim really did wonder, though, if he had some prior knowledge of him. It was almost like he had expected to see him one day.

About a month after Jim noticed the closed window, He was reading the Lakeshore News Journal. He always checked the obituaries to see if anyone he knew had died. As he looked down the column, his eyes froze on the name he saw before him. Roy Harding had died! It seemed so strange. Jim felt this deep feeling of loss. For so long Roy had been an important part of his life. Jim hadn't seen him since he had the drinks in his shop so long ago. He had served time in prison for something. Jim had guessed it was drug trafficking. He never bothered to find out. He learned though, that Roy and his new wife had moved across the street from his old home in Lakeshore, but he had never seen him there. Jim knew he had to attend his funeral for two reasons. One of them was the chance that Betsy Lee might be there.

After Jim met James Taylor and realized Betsy Lee was living in the area, He decided to do a computer search for information about her. What he discovered was interesting. She had not married until nineteen ninety eight, just eight years ago. Unless he didn't have all the information, she hadn't married for twenty-four years after he had seen her last. This made his heart wonder. Jim learned she lived in a condo in Lakeshore now. He went there one day. It was one of those secure types. Jim went so far as to know she lived there and left. He wouldn't just walk up. He would communicate with her before trying to meet again, if that was, in fact, possible.

Dorothy didn't want to go to Roy's funeral with Jim so he went alone. He was there early so he signed the register first. Yes, with that bold stroke he had learned from his Uncle Oliver. Jim noticed it stood out on top of the page. As he walked down the aisle toward a seat, he noticed that the casket was not present. Then, looking to the left of the center, Jim saw this large, life size mounted photograph. He felt this warm surge flow through him. His heart skipped a beat. It was the picture of Betsy Lee and Roy that stood by the counter in their shop. Jim was filled with deep emotion. It was like going back to a distant place in time. It was like seeing a lost loved one that one never expected to see again. No, it wasn't her person, but it was her. Jim had but one wrinkled old newspaper print of Betsy Lee, long since put away. He waited patiently as one after another the visitors came. Betsy Lee did not come. The service began. The preachers did their job as usual, but then came the testimony of his sister. She recollected important events in Roy's life. At one point she mentioned that even though he was married to a beautiful woman he had tried to put his family first back then. Jim could feel the emotion well up in him. He knew Roy loved her and first. When she mentioned how Roy struggled with divorce, Jim clenched his teeth and tears formed in his eyes. He began to ask for forgiveness. He knew it was way too late. Jim knew he had not taken Betsy Lee away from him, but he knew he had an influence on the outcome of their marriage. Betsy Lee was in Jim's thoughts again, though the memory of her had never left.

Jim never responded to any of what he *thought* were Angela's "advances," and he really did not understand completely their purpose or her intent. It was as if she was driven by some external motivation to press him to leave his wife or by some other consideration that may have concerned her children. Jim thought at one time she may have had a dream or a spiritual vision about something that concerned him. Jim could never understand what was behind her unusual behavior and why she could never talk to him openly about it. No one would ever talk to him, but plenty of people seemed to know something about it and were trying to help her. Jim sent another e-mail to the preacher. He mentioned in that letter a hope for resolution. He suggested it would be a great Christian witness for everyone, if two people could rally behind the love of Christ and become Christian friends and work for the glory of God. Jim mentioned that he was still waiting patiently for the person to express directly to him any complaint. Below is the e-mail Jim sent.

Fri. Sept 2006 08:36:27 -0700 (PDT).
From: Jim Josephson
Subject: T. W. Bishop
To: "Brother Steve Faircloth"

When you see T.W. this Sunday, would you tell him that I had previously planned a trip out of town this Sunday, and that I love him very much. The love of God will see us through these difficult times. I am not guiltless, but this whole thing is innocent from both sides. The Lord is on both sides. There is no satanic element here other than the evil that might be created in other people's minds by their own imaginations.

I pray for the spiritual health of this church. I always have. I pray for you and your leadership. I love the "Church" which of course is the people, but magnified by the beauty of the sanctuary and the holiness that is there when Christians come to share their lives in worship. I ask for your forgiveness for the difficulty I have caused you, though I never meant to. If necessary, I will remove myself from the church, if this will insure the health of the church, but what a blessing it would be for all to see, if they could see two Christians rally behind the love of Christ and become friends and workers for Christ, which is what they really are anyway.

I have spoken to no one other than T. W. About any of this and no one, I mean no one, has spoken directly to me about any of this. As I have said before, I am blind, like General Lee at Gettysburg. If I am right, you are aware of all of this, and I thank you for the guiding hand you have offered.

Christian love always,

Jim Josephson

After this e-mail tensions eased a little. Jim would see her occasionally in passing, and they would greet each other cordially. Jim saw the children often, engaged in their activities, but he never talked to them other than to say hello. She had accepted the position as leader of the Women on Mission for the church and Dorothy was a member of this group. Jim thought "Uh Oh! Trouble here." After a couple of meetings, Jim asked Dorothy about her work with the women. She was very positive. She said Angela was going to be a good leader and over all she was pleased with everything. Jim was a little surprised but very pleased about this. Dorothy said they were working on the angel tree for Christmas and that everyone should participate. The angel tree is a Christmas tree with angel tags hung all over it. Each angel tag is a child that has been identified as needy. A person selects an angel and buys a present for the child listed. It is a great work for Christmas. After services Angela would stand at a desk and help register people's selections of angels. Jim walked up after one service to the desk. A line of people were waiting to be registered. Jim was in a hurry so he spoke to Angela about getting an angel. "I'm going to get an angel but not now. I am going to get one later." Jim said. He never thought twice about what he said. Jim was talking about angels on the tree. People were standing all around them. She replied, "I'm going to bring you a bunch of angels." "*You* are going to bring *me* a bunch of angels?" Jim questioned. "Yes," she said, "I am going to bring you a bunch of angels." Jim thought quickly, "Maybe she is talking about the angels on the tree. Dorothy is working with her." "No," He realized, reflecting on past experiences.—"It is her children. She is talking about bringing me her children!" One cannot imagine how one's mind can race through months and years of experiences and unanswered questions so quickly. Jim blurted out in a moment of weakness, "Bring them on then.", and walked off. Jim wondered afterward if this reactionary and reckless comment would be taken by Angela as a commitment of a sort. The next time Jim saw her and her friend, they were all smiles. She was jubilant and happy. He thought, "Goodness, I believe she really thinks I am going to leave my wife and family and take her and her children." Strange things began to happen, though. The preacher in a message spoke about improper worship. Her demeanor soured. She looked dejected and sad. The children disappeared. Jim didn't see any of them for weeks. He knew then that third parties were somehow manipulating and monitoring this situation, but he was blind. Jim knew nothing. No one was talking to him. He was broken hearted, grief ridden and confused, but he knew he cared for her wellbeing. After all, she was the daughter of a man and woman Jim dearly loved.

Jim noticed after these events that Angela's Mom and Dad seemed to be withdrawing their attention toward him. No longer did they come and sit with him at dinner on Wednesday or the prayer meeting that followed. Once at Sunday night service a strange thing happened. Angela's mom sat down close to Jim, and Jim said to her, "You folks know I love you, don't you?" She replied, "We love you no matter which way this turns out." It was as if she thought Jim knew what was really going on. He wondered if she meant what he thought she did. T. W. was reluctant to sit with Jackie because she was so close to him. Eventually he did. Angela was not there that night. Her husband, Mark, was supposed to deliver the benediction at the end of the service. When he stepped up to do so, T. W. and Jackie got up and left the sanctuary. Jim could not understand this behavior. He thought. "Why were they obviously objecting to their son in law?" He figured they were objecting because they could not get Mark to act in any way against him, now that they knew he would not commit to Angela and her children. As a matter of fact, Jim had expected them to withdraw after they realized he would not commit to their daughter. Everyone knew they had an emotional connection. What they didn't know was the extent of it. What Jim desired in Angela was a Christian relationship that would do great things for the Church. He always wanted to explain this to Angela and her mom and dad, but it would just never happen. Something would always prevent it. He knew this could not be done with two people who could not keep their promises, whose oaths were not good. Some other way for good to come of this would have to be found. Jim prayed for the resolution of this situation and that the love of God would fill them.

T. W. was away one Sunday, and Dr. Jay Cumberland, Minister of Administration, substituted for him as teacher of the Older Men's Class that Jim attended. Dr. Cumberland was a recent addition to the staff, and this was the first time Jim had the opportunity to meet him. His teaching approach was much different from T. W's. He was a professional talker it seemed. He started talking, or lecturing, at the beginning and seemed to never stop to allow any input from the members of the class. Eventually Jim did interrupt to insert a comment, and this opened up some conversation and exchange of ideas. He had at one time been a pastor, and he said that preaching was what he was called to do and liked the most. Well, preaching was what he was doing in this teaching situation. He seemed to appreciate Jim's comments and realized that he had knowledge enough about the scriptures and the history of the church to exchange ideas or even to challenge some of his points on his level. As Jim looked around the class, he realized that most of the other members were bored with Dr. Cumberland's high class "lecturing". T. W. was a great teacher, and they were not impressed with this approach. Toward the end of the session he began to talk about some of his duties as Minister of Administration at Lakeview Baptist Church. Some of the older members wondered why we needed to pay another person salary to do such a job. We were paying large sums of money to several people to perform professional duties that they really felt should be done by members as a ministry to the church. The size of the church had become so large, however, that full time duties were necessary in several areas of the ministry of the church, and people were salaried to perform them. As he discussed his duties, he injected a point about how certain things were openly "going on" in the church and they needed to be addressed and stopped. They had no place in the church, he said. He didn't comment further, but this was said in such a way as to make Jim believe he was talking about what was happening between Angela and him in the church. Jim was sure he was letting him know he was going to address this activity. Jim knew that many of the leaders of the church were aware of this activity, and he really felt that it had become discussion at various closed session meetings of the officers of the church. In fact, Jim really felt T. W. was pressuring certain leaders of the church as well as Angela's husband to discipline him for it. After this meeting in the class, Mr. Cumberland and Jim became friends as they casually greeted and talked to each other, which seemed to be quite often. He never specifically mentioned to Jim anything about what was happening, but he could sense Dr. Cumberland was checking on things and evaluating him for his own personal knowledge. He was a jolly and friendly person to be around, and they became friends with one another. As he and Jim became more acquainted, Jim asked him why the music on Wednesday night had stopped. Jim explained he loved that part of the service and most of the other people did also. Dr. Cumberland said he would check into it and see, he did not know. Jim also told him about his time Wednesday night after the dinner that he had set aside to read the bible. Jim explained this was why he came there early, and he had been doing this since he came to this church. Dr. Cumberland soon began to realize the depths of Jim's feelings about his faith and began to see Jim as a man of character and integrity. Jim realized Dr. Cumberland's views about what he was led to believe about him (Jim thought T. W. had probably briefed him) had begun to change, but this was just conjecture on his part. This was what some (particularly the minister of music) of the other leaders in the church had needed to do, rather than just ostracizing him, because of his views of science and evolution and his questionable involvement with Angela. This situation was like Jesus and the Pharisees. Those particular leaders had their opinion of Jim, and they could not love him. Jim has weaknesses, but his heart is filled with genuine love for people and for the spirit of Jesus. It is easy for him to love, even his enemies, it always has been. When someone needs genuine love and caring Jim can give it. When someone really touches the depths of his heart and need, it connects to the very essence of his being, to that place where Jesus lives, to the hope of his soul.

One Wednesday night Jim was sitting in the sanctuary after the supper reading as he had related to Jay (Dr. Cumberland). Angela came in and sat down two pews up from him with one of her friends. Jay was there that night, and Jim had greeted him previously. Jim looked up as Angela sat down. She had turned sideways in the pew with her arm on the back facing her friend, but she was looking around directly at Jim. She would not look off, and they engaged the nonverbal exchange of feelings and emotion that had been happening for so long. It was so obvious that it was embarrassing to Jim, because he could not help but express his feeling, and he looked off. She would not, however. She would not turn around and just kept looking at him with feeling. Jim would look down to read and after a few moments of reading, he would look up and she was still turned around looking at him. Jim tried to ignore this, but it was very difficult to do. It fulfilled the need to communicate within him, and he could not help it. Eventually, he just looked down to read and would not look up. About this time a paper wad about the size of a baseball hit him on the shoulder and fell to the seat beside him. Jim paused for a moment and did not look up as he contemplated what had happened. He thought to himself, "This is a ridiculous insult. If this came from the balcony, I am going up there to reprimand who did it and whatever happens will happen." Only a moment had passed and when Jim looked around, he saw Jay standing at the end of his pew laughing. Angela was still turned around facing him across the pew. Jim said to Jay, "Oh, *you* threw that!" He picked it up and threw it back at him. "It's a good thing it didn't come from the balcony," Jim said. "I was headed up there!" They laughed together at this, and Jim knew this was Jay's way of telling him that what was happening was not right, but he knew then Jim was not the one instigating it. They remained friends and Jay never spoke to him about this "problem" that needed to be corrected because Jim thought he had realized he was not "coming on" to this lady. She was deeply involved in this herself. No officer of the church, at any time, ever approached Jim or ever spoke to him about being responsible for anything concerning this problem.

As time unfolded, husband was reappearing. Jim noticed one evening she had a new car, a red SUV. When he saw her again she was wearing the red lipstick. Jim began to wonder if she had another suitor somewhere. He had seen a young divorced man at church one time and could see that her attention was divided between them, and she seemed bothered. All kinds of scenarios ran through his mind in an attempt to understand her behavior. Had she had an extra marital relationship before? Was she really the little angel he thought she was? Did she have some kind of bi-polar condition? What was the underlying motivation that had caused her to pursue him so strongly? The confusing circumstances and lack of knowledge had caused these negative questions to unfold in his mind. She started coming back to Wednesday night prayer meetings with her girl friends. One in particular seemed to be with her a lot. It was like they were mentoring her.

Jim had always wanted to sing in the choir, but Dorothy had requested he not sing. Jim knew he could not sing in the choir until this problem between them could be resolved. He knew he needed to get her input to see if he would be a problem for her. Would she quit if he came to the choir to sing? Their attraction was always present, but their relationship was strained. Jim knew he had to talk to her about many things. He really needed some answers. Did she really expect him to leave his wife when she went to Dads, without any communication at all between them? It hardly seemed possible. Did he not hear, that fateful night, important parts of the conversation she had with her dad that were meant for him? What did she mean by the comment, "I am going to bring you a bunch of angles?" What would her dad think if he knew of all of the unusual behavior toward him?

It appeared one Wednesday night that her friend was coaxing her to talk to Jim. She had come to the vestibule where Jim had been, accompanied by her friend. Jim had left to go to the restroom. When Jim opened the door to come out, she was alone, standing there hesitantly, but turned to go back into the church. Jim tried to stop her. He called out to her, but she kept going. He followed her into the sanctuary calling to her, but she would not stop. As Jim did this he realized he had openly revealed his interest in her. A sense of relief came over him. Choir members waiting in the choir were watching. Jim had followed her right out into the sanctuary, in front of God and everybody in an attempt to talk to her, but she would not comply. Jim really felt good about what he had done. At last Jim had admitted without reservation that he had a legitimate and open interest in her. He stopped in the middle of the church, turned around and went back to the vestibule. The sanctuary has two large double door entries from the vestibule. The other sanctuary door was closed. Jim stepped behind that door and looked through the small window for her in the choir. She saw him, and a big smile erupted on her face. As Jim stepped back from the door, her girl friend came through the other open door. She looked at him and shrugged. Jim shrugged at her as she went into the bathroom. "What did all of this mean?" Jim wondered.

Later on in the vestibule of the church after a church service, Jim stopped the lady that had accompanied Angela that night. Her husband was standing with her as he approached her. "Pardon me. I am Jim Josephson. I saw you with Angela the other night when I tried to talk to her. I have been having trouble communicating with Angela and wondered if you knew anything that would help me resolve this difficulty." "No, I don't know anything about any of this and don't know of anything I can do to help you." She said. "Thank you for taking time to speak with me." Jim replied. He glanced at her husband as they parted. He was conciliatory but had a concerned look on his face. You would think they could see that Jim really didn't have anything to hide. It seemed no one would talk to him about any of this. No one ever offered any help toward resolving this difficult situation. All of Jim's communication with the people involved and some of the leaders were ignored. Jim was left to stand alone.

Jim knew for his own health he had to resolve this somehow. Somehow he had to communicate with her. They had to talk to one another. He needed to know what her intent in all of this was. Jim always expected she would come to him at some time and talk this out, but it never happened. He always wondered if he was being manipulated, if it was entrapment, but he could not for the life of him figure it out. Jim decided to try to communicate, knowing it was a risk. He sent an e-mail to her computer at school where she worked. Jim waited several days for a reply but never received one. This is the e-mail that Jim sent.

To: Angela Davis
From: Jim Josephson

Angela, I have a religious writing I would like for you to have. Under the circumstances, I do not know what is appropriate to do. I would like to send it to you. Is it ok? I would not for the world offend you in any way. Tell Stephanie hello for me. I was her teacher some years ago.

Thanks,

Jim

Jim got no response from this e-mail. About a week after this on a Saturday, he met her husband on an isolated isle in Home Depot. Jim did not hesitate. He walked right to him and greeted him in a friendly manner. He was also friendly in his greeting to Jim. Jim knew he had to communicate something. He said, "Mark, you know I love you, don't you? You might not believe this, but it is true." Mark replied, "Yes, I believe you. I believe you because of the way your boys always were." Everyone loved Jim's boys. They were always gentlemanly, courteous and kind and were respected. Jim added, "You know it's not wrong to care about someone is it?" "No, it's not." He said. "As a matter of fact it would be wrong not to care, wouldn't it?" Jim added. "Yes, It would really be wrong not to." He admitted. They conversed casually for a few moments after this. He mentioned that they (meaning, he and Angela) had visited a couple they had briefly talked about. Jim thought this was to emphasize they were together. Jim really did not know what their family life was like. It appeared to him they always lived together except for the move to dad's house for the construction. If there was ever a separation Jim was not aware of it. Angela had insinuated this with her behavior toward Jim, but he never knew of an actual separation. Jim knew her relationship with their daughters seemed strained. He really felt they were having difficulty, but he did not know the extent of it. Surely Mark must have questioned her about their relationship or either he was a party to it. After their first encounters and emotional contact, he had been removed more or less from her activity that Jim could observe. This could have been intentional. He seemed to move in and out of the picture, but Jim could never know why. No one was talking to him.

The Church had nominated new deacons and was going to install them the next Sunday night. One of them had befriended Jim's granddaughter when she was in school, and they were friends. He had also been very kind and friendly with Jim. He was the one who prayed with Jim in the closet in the dream. Jim went to the ordination ceremony that night. A reception was held afterward in the fellowship hall. Jim attended the reception, greeted and congratulated the deacons, and sat down to converse with a member of his Sunday school class. Shortly afterward, he saw Mark, Angela, and their three daughters come in together. They almost appeared as if they were greeting each other. She was dressed well, had on a skirt and blouse, and interestingly, black full length stockings. Jim knew he had a chance to act. He walked up to Mark from behind, put his arm around him, and greeted him. Mark responded cordially, and Jim asked him, "Can I ask your wife a question?" Mark said, "Yes, Go ahead." Jim walked over to Angela and when he looked at her to ask the question, their eyes met and there was that spark, that spark of the eternal spring! Her eyes never wavered, they stayed locked on his. He could have just embraced her. Jim asked her the question, "If I join the choir will you quit?" "W'y no," She said, "Why would I quit?" "That's great," Jim said, "That's what I needed to know." There was laughter and someone spoke out, "What did he ask?" And she said, "If he joined the choir would I quit." Jim heard someone else say, "Why did he ask that question?" Angela turned to Jim and said, "We want you to join the choir. Brother Rob will be glad to have you sing. We will look for you next Wednesday." Jim replied, "I will try, but my hearing is bad and I don't know how I will do." She said, "Are you kidding? Have you heard our men sing?" This open rebuke of the men offended Jim, and he was taken aback. He said, "I will see you Wednesday." Jim started back to his chair when he thought of something else. He turned back to Angela and asked, "Did you get the e-mail I sent?" She said, "No, I didn't. When did you send it?" "About a week ago." Jim said. "Resend it." She said, "You can send it to my home e-mail address. I will give it to you." "No, I won't send it to your home address. I'll resend it to your school. " Jim had done this so that others there would see that his communication to her was open and above board. Jim re-sent the e-mail, and she allowed him to send her the religious writing. At the end of the Psalm-like poem, Jim wrote this comment.

> *This was written, unknowingly, upon the 50th anniversary of the state of Israel. And then, shortly afterward, it snowed upon Israel. Because of that, even if just a coincidence, it has been dear to me. I hope we can communicate more. We need to. I apologize to you for anything that I have done that might have offended you or let you down and ask for your forgiveness. If this is acceptable, let me know.*

Jim never received any answer or comment about this e-mail. She never communicated in any way what Jim asked was acceptable. This bothered him a lot. He wondered why she wouldn't respond. Jim went to choir practice that next Wednesday. Angela and Brother Rob, the Minister of Music, were not there. Jim did the best he could to keep up. Some of the choir members helped him get organized. Jim couldn't hear himself sing very well and he couldn't hear the director's instructions. It was very difficult. Jim followed the music fairly well but could not sing out. At the end they gave him the applause of welcome. He was embarrassed. He knew he could not go through with this under the circumstances. It appeared to Jim Angela and Rob had missed practice on purpose.

Angela and Jim exchanged a couple of e-mails. She was encouraging and said that the minister of music really wanted him to sing. Jim explained about his hearing loss. He thought about trying to stick with the choir, but knowing what he did about the situation between Angela and himself, he realized it was hopeless.

He was there for the wrong reasons. He was trying to engage Angela so as to find out what was going on between them. Jim wanted to be there for the right reasons, but nevertheless, he was there for the wrong ones. Jim sent an e-mail to the choir explaining that he would not be able to sing in the choir at this time. Maybe he would rejoin later. One thing about this really bothered Jim. He was personally acquainted with many of the choir members. There were over seventy members in the choir. Not one sent Jim an e-mail in response, and not one spoke to him about it. Did they really think he was pursuing this lady? What had she told them? Jim felt that many of them knew there was an emotional connection. Were they just trying to ignore a troublesome problem? Was Angela personally just trying to "save" an old evolutionary biologist (in the fundamentalist view an evolutionary biologist was violating an important doctrine of the Church) and they knew that? Whatever the reason, Jim was hurt a little, and it made him reassess his behavior.

A revival was approaching. It was to begin the next weekend and extend into the next week. Everyone was trying to prepare themselves spiritually. Jim was working that weekend. He attended the last night of the revival. Angela sang in an ensemble with some of her friends in the choir. Jim tried hard not to look directly at her though this was next to impossible. When their eyes did meet, Jim could see the emotion begin to well up. He looked away and would not look directly at her any more. They finished the piece and it was beautiful. The revival preacher then preached a very fitting revival message for their church. It was about kinds of Christians. He used metaphors as examples of the kinds of Christians. Some were animals. He closed with an eagle. In the last parallel he drew, he used the mating ritual. He related how the female eagle would fly up very high, to the highest she could reach and the male prospects would follow her. She would have a twig in her beak and would drop it. As it fell toward the ground, the remaining male eagle would dive down and catch the twig. This ritual would continue for days until the female eagle was satisfied with her mate. Then from the highest level she could reach, she would turn over upside down and the male eagle would join her on top. They would mesh their talons together like clasped hands between the fingers and flutter to the ground singing songs to each other. When they did this they were mated for life and no other eagle would take either ones place. When he finished this beautiful parallel to Christian bonding of man and woman, Jim looked over toward the other side of the church. He could not see Angela. Jim did not know how she had reacted, but he saw one of her friends. She was weeping. Tears were streaming down her face. She knew all along about Angela and Jim. She had been beside her in the serving line that night. Jim knew she was happily married. He really thought those tears were for Angela. Why had this minister chosen this sensitive emotional parallel in a church setting like this? Was this coincidence? It hardly seemed likely. Jim had to bring this heartbreak to a close. The next day he wrote this final e-mail.

To: Angela Davis
From: Jim Josephson

Angela,

I know I have embarrassed you here lately. I apologize for that. It seems that the things that are the most important to me are the things that get misdirected. What I wrote to your dad for you, Angela, is true. I think you know that. Will you trust me? Can I trust you to know things I must tell you? You have no need to fear me. I am not the evil one regardless of what you may have been told. You may doubt my intentions, but they are innocent and only what you will accept. I have been blind because I never knew for sure what was happening. I knew what had happened to me. No one, including you, would talk directly to me about it. If it's impossible to be anything else for you, I want to at least be a Christian friend to you and all of your family. It would be a real tragedy if this could not happen.

Jim

Jim did not get an answer. Several days passed. Jim knew that Angela had not been in her usual places. He began to look for her. He couldn't find her. Late one night, her car finally arrived at home. Jim still never heard from her. He began to worry. Finally he got enough courage to call her dad. He had been sick several days before, and Jim had called him to check on his condition. When he answered the phone, Jim said, "This is Jim. How are you doing T. W.?" "I am doing fine." Jim could hear a little antagonism in his voice as he spoke in the background to someone there with him. "It's Jim Josephson, he's on the phone." Jim took a deep breath. He asked, "How is Angela?" "Is she ok?" "No, she's not." he replied. And there was a moment of silence. "Can you talk about it?" Jim asked. "I would rather talk about it in person, but I will anyway. Angela came over to the house the other night almost in tears and wanted to know about this letter I had. Angela said she didn't feel comfortable in the church she grew up in anymore. She said you had sent her this e-mail. Why did you do this Jim? We had agreed to let this drop. At one time Jim, I thought you were a man of character and principle, but now I can't understand why you would send an e-mail to a married woman like that!" Jim injected, "I haven't done anything wrong T. W." "You don't think it's wrong to send an e-mail like that to a married woman!?" "Don't you know you will have to answer to God for this!?" "This has been going on for a long time, T. W.! It's not like I just sent this thing!" Then Jim said something he wasn't sure of, "You've just been waiting for me to make a mistake. I'm not going to try to defend myself to you T. W. You wouldn't believe me anyway!" He replied angrily, "You'll answer to God for this! "I don't want you to have any more contact with Angela, none whatsoever. No contact with her children, none at all. I'm disappointed in you Jim. You've got a problem!" Jim returned heatedly, "What's her children got to do with this T. W.!? "I'm not the only one that's got a problem!!" Bang! He hung up the receiver!

Jim was saddened, deeply hurt and troubled with this conversation. What he had sworn he would not let happen in the beginning had happened and he could not do anything to stop it.

Why had Angela not trusted him and talked to him personally? He would have been able to solve this difficult situation quietly. Jim knew he had to discuss the nature of their encounters with her. He also needed to explain his intent. Jim wanted to openly and frankly know her feelings and her intent and what she might have experienced that had caused her to pursue him so relentlessly. She would never talk to him about this before and she wasn't going to talk to him now. Her actions were just too confusing to Jim. She must have been really thinking about leaving her husband and dad was resisting her. T. W. knew nothing good could come from this. But as always, Jim could never know the truth. Why would a dad need to tell a person who was obviously not threatening to his daughter that he needed to have no contact with her? She is a forty year old woman and could stop the advance of any reasonable man if something like that was happening. What *did* her children have to do with this? Were they trying to protect her from herself and what she might do? Jim didn't know. This was always the problem. Jim had seen enough tears and smiles from her women friends, hard looks from her husband's men friends, and curious behavior on the part of the minister and officers of the church not to realize they knew something about this relationship. Jim felt Angela was withholding from him something she knew about or had experienced that others had knowledge of. He also wondered if he had been set up. Jim couldn't think of anything he could do differently as far as his activities at the church were concerned because he had never gone out of his way to meet her, to touch her or anything like that. The only contact he had ever had with her children was to say hello in church. It would mean he would eventually have to quit attending this church. He wondered if this might not really be what T. W. wanted all of the time. Once in Sunday school after Angela went back home, T. W. had mentioned open adultery in the church and how the church needed to speak to this problem. He did not use names; he just slid this into his lesson and knew that Jim would know what he was talking about. Jim was tempted to ask him, if he was talking about, one way adultery, or two way adultery, but he didn't.

Chapter Twelve

All of the leaders knew Jim was an evolutionary biologist. He had taught it for thirty-five years. Jim had informed them in a written letter to the officers of the church. He never pressed his views in Dad's Sunday school class, but T. W. was forever prodding him with it. He presented things he believed were absolute truth that he knew Jim questioned, but Jim would never engage in argument. He loved him too much. Jim would inject ideas here and there but always embellished with the love and teachings of Jesus as best he could understand them. He didn't have to consider long about what to do with this situation, because Saturday evening when he and his family were together at home, the phone rang. Dorothy answered the phone. She turned to Jim and said, "It's Mark Davis. He wants to talk to you." Jim took the phone and Mark politely said there could be a problem between their families and he wanted to stop it before it got out of hand. He wanted to talk to him at church the next day. Jim was actually relieved. At last someone was going to talk to him, what he had wanted and what had been needed for so long. Jim agreed to meet with him. The next day Jim waited for him in the designated place to arrive. Through all the years he had been at Lakeview, he had not really felt accepted by some members. Many were leaders, and the places they did most of their work seemed strangely "off limits" to him. Not that he could not frequent those places, but when he did he would get a feeling he was intruding into their space, and did not feel comfortable there. He had those feelings as he waited. He knew it had something to do with his views of evolution. They were well known. Once Ted Barnett, the minister of students, approached him, and in good faith and respect asked him to join his "Creation" class at discipleship training. Jim replied, "You wouldn't want an evolutionary biologist in your Creation class, would you?" Ted was a little startled because Jim was so frank, (he already knew Jim's views before he asked) but replied, "Oh no, you are welcome to come. We like to discuss things and talk about different views." Jim knew he would get nowhere there but in an argument, so he did not attend. The preacher, Brother Steve Faircloth, came by while Jim was waiting and they talked. Jim asked what he could do, or should do. He offered to make a public statement and apology. Brother Steve said there would be "no need" for that. Then he said something that bothered Jim. He said he didn't know much about this and that the minister of music said he knew nothing about this. Jim knew if the minister of music had said that to him, he was telling an untruth. He may have meant just the phone call, but he knew about this problem he and Angela had from the very beginning. He was a player in it, in that he tried to manipulate people according to his judgment about what he thought was going on. Mark finally came. He was pleasant, cordial and didn't seem angry. Jim mentioned they needed a third party to attend, an officer of the church. Mark is a deacon himself. He agreed. Jim suggested Dr. Jay Cumberland. Mark said no, he couldn't do it. Jim thought he knew why. Mark said he would go and find someone. He came back later and had the Minister of Education with him, Ted Barnett. They moved into the study and seated themselves. Mark sat squarely in front of Jim, and Ted sat on his right. There was no table, just an open room. Mark began discussing his complaint. Jim interrupted. Mark asked Jim to let him give his view in its entirety first, and Jim agreed. His complaint was Jim had sent this e-mail and had upset his wife. He also mentioned the choir incident and said they were puzzled at why Jim had done this. He also mentioned, quite frankly, that Angela had said she had no attraction for Jim, and Mark knew this because they shared everything they did and discussed everything freely. He said he thought Jim had a problem and needed to address it. When it came Jim's time to speak, He began by saying this wasn't an isolated incident. Events pertaining to this problem had surfaced at least four years ago. Brother Ted interrupted with, "Four years ago?" Jim said yes four years or more ago and went on. He told them how her mother and father had confronted him about his (advances) eye contact that was offending Angela. Her mother and dad never mentioned names directly, but they inferred that something was wrong with his behavior. He mentioned how he had tried to resolve it then when her dad had confronted him in Sunday school. Jim related how the minister of music had come by and said "Congratulations", how the singing had stopped on Wednesday night, how the couples quit coming, how Mark sat on the back row while his wife sat up front, how he as a husband had disappeared, how Jim thought Angela and others were praying for him, the negative vibes at Wednesday night dinner. Jim explained to them he thought all of this was because Angela felt like he was offending her with his "eye" contact or non-verbal communication. Jim never mentioned any of her amorous reactions toward him or any of what Jim thought were Angela's advances. He never mentioned the letters and contact he had made with Angela's dad and the preacher. He explained the e-mails and choir incident as an attempt on his part to resolve this difficult situation, which of course it was, with the amorous parts omitted. This seemed to go well with Mark, that is, Jim did not accuse Angela of anything. Mark began to explain to Jim that he had a perception problem, that none of this was really related. No singing on Wednesday night had been a staff decision he said. He suggested Jim needed to address this "paranoia" that he had. Jim interrupted with, "I don't have any paranoia. I don't think anyone is out to get me. I know what paranoia is. I studied counseling and psychotherapy in college. I know about schizophrenia, multiple personality, paranoia and bi-polar condition." When Jim said, bi-polar condition, Jim "saw" Mark's mind hesitate for an instant, because Jim was reading his feelings constantly, a skill he had learned long ago. Jim had wondered about things like this concerning Angela before. Brother Ted injected, "No, not paranoia, but just a misinterpretation or misunderstanding of events. Mark said he thought Jim should receive some counseling. Jim knew most of this pressure was coming from Dad. This is what he expected. Jim said he wasn't objectionable to counseling. He would do anything to resolve this difficulty. "I wouldn't be here with my head on the chopping block if I had an ulterior motive, would I?" Jim injected. As the discussion came to a close, Mark began giving Jim some directives, the same ones dad had given. He was to have no contact with Angela. He was to have no contact with his children. Jim interrupted indignantly, "What's your children got to do with this? I taught thirty-five years in the public school and you could count on one hand the problems I had with students. I had good relations with my students. I loved my students and they loved me. Many of these students were girls. On my last year of teaching, I had a biology II class that was largely girls. As the year approached an end, the last year of my teaching, I was sitting at my desk and my students were working at their desks. It was quiet in the room as everyone worked. I looked up and one of my female students was looking at me. She said, "We love you, Mr. Josephson." I replied, somewhat broken with emotion, "I love all of you, too but not"—I was interrupted with; "We know. We understand, Mr. Josephson." "And this reminds me, once Joseph and I were in Arby's for lunch. Some people that I did not know came in with several children. When I looked over where they were seated, I saw that one of them was your child. When she saw me, her face flushed, tears began to well in her eyes and she got up, went to the bathroom and didn't come out. Why did she do that Mark?" I asked. "Was this my paranoia? I had never even spoken to your child before except maybe 'Hi' or something." Jim noticed brother Ted began to listen. Jim urged him to check out things from the other side. Jim had set Mark back because he knew about this incident. Jim took the initiative. "One Sunday, Mark, you were taking up the collection. When you got to the pew where I was sitting, you extended your hand to me and I shook it. Why did you do this, Mark? I asked, Why me out of all of the others?" He just said, "We often do this." Jim thought he knew at the time why he did it. He was thanking him for not taking advantage of a situation that Jim himself did not completely understand. The subject changed to values. Mark said that anytime he sent an e-mail to a married woman he sent a copy to her husband so no misunderstandings would occur. Jim said he thought that was a good idea. A discussion of normal and abnormal behavior came up. Jim didn't really know why he chose this, but he knew if Angela's behavior was not entrapment, then she was trying to steal him from his wife, and he said, "You know, if you lived in a group where everyone was a stealer, stealing would be normal." Jim turned and looked straight at Brother Ted and said, "Like the Black Foot Indian." He saw Ted flinch back. "I'm twenty percent 'Black Foot Indian'!" He exclaimed. Jim quipped quickly, "Have you stolen any horses lately?" Jim did not know he was part Black Foot Indian. He was as surprised as Ted was. Things began to break up then. Jim said he would check into the counseling recommendation. Brother Matt said he would e-mail him the information. They departed on good terms. Jim left in his truck and went home. Of course, he was questioned by Dorothy and Joseph. She knew why he went there, in part. Jim said it was because he had offended Angela. He explained what Mark and her dad had admonished him to do. Gradually and carefully, over the next weeks, Jim began in subtle ways to disclose his real difficulty.

A few days after the meeting, Brother Steve Faircloth called him with the name and address of a counselor. Jim took the opportunity to expand his point of view. Jim was sure he knew much more about this than he was disclosing. Some of it he could not disclose because of confidentiality. Only lately had Jim thought about this. He always wondered why he wouldn't communicate with him about something he obviously knew and Jim didn't. He couldn't. Now he could understand why the preacher's messages were laced with "clues" for him to decipher. Jim really believed they were there. He didn't think it was "read in" on his part. After thanking Brother Steve for the help and information, Jim related to him, "I only told part of the story. Angela either really cared for me and was making advances toward me or she was trying to entrap me, and I could never figure this out for sure. It seemed as if some religious experience she had was motivating her to pursue me. I know for a fact she was emotionally involved with me." Brother

Steve replied. "You know Jim sometimes intentions can be misread. She is such an outgoing person." "I know but I don't think that is the case here. I know things you don't know. You know things I don't know. T. W. knows things we both don't know. The Minister of Music knows things we all don't know but God knows it all." At that they ended the conversation.

Jim called T. W. back after this. The phone rang and T. W. said hello. "This is Jim T. W. I just called to see if it was ok with you if I came back to your Sunday school class again." "I don't have the authority to tell anyone what to do in church. You can come back if you want to." He said. "Well T. W., will you welcome me back?" "I didn't say that." He said. "Well I'll be going T. W. Goodbye and Tell Jackie I said hello." Jim wondered how he would handle this.

Jim decided to withdraw from church for a while. He took his grandson to Wednesday night dinner and left him. He picked him up after the church service. He did not attend church for a few Sundays. The first Sunday Jim came back, Dorothy, her mother, and step father also attended. Joseph was not there. They all sat on the same pew. Angela was present in the choir and everything seemed to go well. Occasionally Angela and Jim would glance at each other. Jim could tell that, deep down, there were some concerns on her part. He saw her smile broadly at someone on the other side of the church. He couldn't tell who it was. They were all tense. Jim knew Dorothy's Mother and Stepfather knew something of this, but what and how much he didn't know. Then everyone stood to sing a church song. Jim sang out and could begin to feel the strong emotion flow. Angela was singing. They glanced at each other. Jim saw the emotion surge in her eyes. He looked off. After the hymn, everyone remained standing for the introduction to the prayer for the offering. Angela's face began to blush. She began fanning herself with her bulletin. She began to cry as the prayer began. Tears were streaming down her cheeks. Dorothy sat down beside Jim as he stood, and began to pray. Jim stood stone faced, too emotionally drained to cry but heartbroken for everyone to the depths of his soul. When the prayer was over, Jim looked up. Angela was gone. So was Ted the officer that had met with Mark and Jim. Brother Steve started the message. He preached a great sermon on true love. He said true love was a spiritual thing that touched the heart of God. He preached from the Old Testament, about Ruth and Boaz, from the book of Ruth. He described vividly how Ruth implemented the principle of Kinsman Redeemer. Jim's heart was moved to wonder. How could he possibly have known about his dream? As church dismissed Jim told Dorothy he would have to go first to the restroom. She said she would be waiting for him there, he wasn't going anywhere without her. When Jim came back Dorothy was waiting. They walked out into an almost empty vestibule. As they walked across the back of the church together, they met Brother Ted. He stopped and greeted them warmly. Jim wondered why he was there, and what Angela had told him because he knew he went out to be with her. Brother Ted turned to Jim and said quite surprisingly, "Great things are going to happen to you over this." "You mean what we talked about?" Jim asked. He said, "Yes, Great things are going to come to you because of it." "Well I have been praying about it." Jim said. "Great things!" Jim reflected to himself. "Great things! I wonder what he means by great things. I wonder what she might have told him."

Jim decided to attend the next Wednesday night dinner. His grandson had homework and could not attend. He went alone. At the meeting with her husband after the discussions, Jim had asked then outright if they were going to sue him. He said no. Jim asked if they were going to "Church" him. They said no. Jim could not understand how he could participate in church activities and have no contact with Angela. He thought, "Well, I won't speak, and I'll keep my distance." This was essentially what he had been doing. As soon as Jim stepped into the door that night, He saw Angela standing in front of him. She was alone. Jim didn't know she was there because her red sport utility vehicle was parked behind the church where it couldn't be seen. Husband and Dad were nowhere to be found. They looked at each other and Jim went on by, without speaking, to the serving line. She stayed back where she was and began talking to a gentleman there. Jim took his dinner and moved on to the table by the wall where he had been sitting for the past year or so. Angela remained for a while talking to the gentleman. Later, Jim noticed she was talking on her cell phone. She moved over into the serving recess and began talking on the wall phone. Jim thought she might be calling to tell her husband and children that he was there. She picked up at least three to-go plates. Jim thought, "Well, She is going to leave because I am here." She carried the to-go plates back to her table and sat down. She did not leave. Jim talked with friends at his table. He noticed Angela get up and start to the front. She came slowly, speaking to people. She turned and walked straight to Jim's table. They looked at each other as she passed as close to the table as she could. Jim waited for her to speak. She did not speak. Jim did not speak. He could not tell what she meant by this. He could not read her intent. It could have been intimidation, but it sure didn't appear to be. He really thought she was trying to say, "It wasn't me, it was them.", but this as always, could have been imagination. She went on by, greeted another lady, and returned to her table. Shortly after that Jim left for the sanctuary as he had always done. After seating himself, he took a hymnal from the holder on the back of the pew. He started thumbing through it. He began to sing to himself the first lines of the old songs he loved so much. Jim didn't notice much else. He just sang the lines of the spirits of the Saints and knew their love of the Christ lived inside of him. After some time of being moved at the lines of the hearts of men poured out long ago, he noticed Angela come in with one of her friends and sit down. She didn't look his way often, just occasionally. After about ten minutes of enumerating the prayer needs for the sick and needy, Brother Steve began the opening prayer. As the prayer was said, Jim noticed someone leaving. He didn't look around. When he finally looked up after the prayer, Angela was gone. Brother Steve began to deliver the prayer study. After a few moments, Angela came back in and sat down with her friend. She turned to her and put her head on her friend's shoulder. She said something to her. She got up and left again. This was the lady that Jim had asked to help him with his difficulty. As she walked down the aisle, Jim noticed Brother Steve hesitate. He momentarily stumbled on a point. He was ashen and troubled. It was obvious. Jim began to be concerned. Who was outside? Did it involve him? Was her dad and husband coming, maybe her brothers? After she left Jim could hear loud talking outside and the sound of children's voices. It really sounded like an argument. It visibly shook Brother Steve, but he continued on until the end of the service. When the service was over, Jim walked outside. No one was around. He left the church and went to his sister's home. After a brief visit, Jim returned to the church. Her red sport utility vehicle was parked openly in the parking lot where he usually parked his truck. She was at choir practice and again Jim was left with many unanswered questions.

Jim went back to the next regular church service. Dorothy was assigned nursery duty, and Joseph did not attend. He had confided with Samuel about this situation about six months prior to this, and Samuel said later that he was not going back to Lakeview. Jim really did not know what it was that made him make that decision, but he made it nevertheless. Jim thought he may have met with someone in authority at the church, but he did not know for sure. He never said so. Jim wondered what they may have told him, if he did. Samuel is just the greatest son. He was really upset with his dad even though Jim tried his best to explain what had happened and what his real intentions were. It was like a spear had been thrust right straight through Jim's heart, and Jim felt he was totally to blame for it. He knew he should have never let this happen or unfold like it did. Samuel loved his dad and had always revered him for what he believed about character, and Jim had let him down. Jim sat alone over in the corner. Well not alone, but without any family present. Angela was not there that Sunday. He went back to the Wednesday night supper the next week. She was not at that activity either or at the prayer meeting. Jim told the preacher when he met him at the prayer meeting that he could not go back to the older men's class after what had happened. Brother Steve's comment was, "Well, you can understand how he feels. It is his daughter." Jim supposed he had erased from his mind all of the correspondence he had sent him. Jim did not respond to his comment although he should have.

Jim decided to go back to Dad's class and see how he would react in an attempt to mend the soured relationship. When he walked into the room, he greeted Mr. Joel, his nephew's father-in-law. He was very glad to see him and said he had been missing him. Jim turned around, and the rest of the men in the class greeted him warmly. He looked at T. W. He could see the resentment in his face and the surprise of his presence there. They had a good lesson. T. W. is a great teacher. He knows how to relate real situations to the lesson, and he involves everyone he can. They were studying about the healing of the blind man in John's Gospel. Jim saw an opportunity to counter some of the criticisms that had arisen around what was happening. Jim asked T. W. could he read a bit of scripture about what some of the leaders of the Jews had thought about Jesus, even though he was filled with the power of God and had just performed a great miracle. T. W. said he could. Jim read John nine; verse twenty-four from the Living Bible. "So for the second time they called in the man who had been blind and told him, 'Give the glory to God, not to Jesus, for we know Jesus is an *evil* person.' " Jim asked the whole class but directed his comment into the eyes of T. W. Bishop; "If they could say this about Jesus, and for Christians he represents God on this earth, What could someone say about and do to just an ordinary old country boy?", meaning T. W., the Minister of Music, and some of the officers of the church, one of which was Angela's husband, although Jim believed he was forced to confront him. To them, nothing Jim could possibly do was of God. He was an interloper and an evolutionary biologist, whose views were askew. No one would include him in trying to solve this problem even though Jim was the one who could have, because he really had no selfish motives. Selfish feelings? Regretfully, yes. Selfish motives? No. Once after this, Jim met T. W. in the vestibule of the church. He openly shunned him, turned from him, and walked away quickly.

Jim went back to another Wednesday night supper with his grandson. After the supper he went to the church sanctuary expecting a regular prayer meeting. It was a special meeting, however, a bible drill for students studying for competition. Kathy,

Angela's youngest daughter, was there. Angela came in and sat on the opposite side of the church between two of her girl friends. Her husband was not there at first. Jim could not see her because she was between the other girls. As he looked across the church, he noticed two men intently staring at him with a stare down expression of contempt. Jim knew this look. He used it on dogs to intimidate them. Jim could take this no longer. He got up from his seat, walked around the back of the pews and straight to the two men sitting there. One man looked away, in a cower response, as Jim approached. The other one was sitting with his wife and children. Jim spoke to him, introducing himself as Jim Josephson, and asked him who he was. He asked him if he had met him at Arby's or one of the restaurants. He said no, he had not met him before. Jim had a little small talk with him and his wife. The intimidation was gone, they laughed together, and he knew he had made a nonverbal statement to them. When he came back around the back of the church to take his seat, he passed T. W. He tensed when Jim passed, and they did not greet each other. T. W. came around and sat one pew up from him, on the other end, in the center of the church. Angela was directly across from him on the other side in the same row of pews, sandwiched between her two girl friends. T. W. and Mark had both instructed him to have no contact with Angela or her children. After a moment her husband came in and sat down between Angela and one of the girls, causing the girl to move over. Everyone watched the drills, and the children were great. What a blessing to have workers willing to take time with children to teach them the ways of Jesus. Angela's daughter was a little nervous at first, not because of the competition but because of Jim's presence. She would glance at him with an apprehensive look. Jim smiled and encouraged her because he loved her too, as the Christian child of Mark and Angela Davis. The competition went well, and the children were dismissed after awards were given to some of the students. The children and their parents went outside, but the service was not over. As Brother Steve began to take over the service for the abbreviated prayer meeting and message, Angela came back in the sanctuary alone. She came down the far right aisle to the pew where her girl friends were sitting. She moved down the pew, passed by her girl friends and sat on the end in plain view of her dad and Jim. It was as if she was making a statement, even with her dad present, that the order to have no contact with her was not hers and was not appropriate. When the service closed, Angela came straight over to her dad and began talking to him. Jim was only a few feet away. She glanced at him, but they never greeted each other. Jim waited for one of them to recognize his presence. He wanted this to happen so much. They did not know how much Jim loved both of them as Christian friends and how much he wanted them to love him as a Christian friend. This did not happen, however, and he reluctantly moved on out to the foyer where some of his friends were talking.

Jim attended the older men's classroom again, probably for the last time. Jim had learned to love these men. They were men who had lived most of their lives searching the scriptures and trying to live as Christians. They were not so-called, "Squares", but seasoned, mature men who also had a grasp of the world as it is out "there". One man, he was in his seventies, and his wife rode motorcycles. He rode even after he had beaten a bout of colon cancer. He is a gracious and humble man. The oldest man in the class is a hard worker in his garden and knows the scriptures quite well. He had been the previous teacher. Jim loved him like he loved his dad and Uncle Oliver. And of course there was Mister Joel, the class secretary-treasurer. He is a hunter with Indian ancestry, a friend and a friend of Jim's family. They always prayed for others, very seldom for themselves. They appreciated Jim, and he loved them for it. The lesson for this secession was on humility. Jim knew this was going to be hard for T. W. because he was there. He hadn't been very humble toward him in solving his problem. Jim wondered how T. W. would handle the lesson. They read some scripture, and T. W. talked about humility. He said, outright, that he wasn't a very humble person. He admitted he liked to get things done. Jim supposed he was referring to the "open" adultery in the church that he said the church needed to address. He had probably solved this himself by forcing Jim to remove himself from the church since the church never approached Jim about it. Jim was sure he had pressured her husband to meet with him and confront him about the e-mail. Jim didn't mind taking the blame, but he knew he was not alone in this. The adultery was a two-way thing if it really was adultery. T. W. asked members of the class to give their interpretation of being humble and demonstrating humility. Several interpretations were given. They reminded everyone that Jesus was humble, and the nature of Christianity was to demonstrate real humility. As the meeting drew to a close, Jim asked T. W. if he could read to the class what the Bible said about real humility. T. W. said he could. Jim read the thirteenth chapter of First Corinthians verses four through seven from the Living Bible. He read clearly and distinctly. Jim put all of the emotion and inflection he could in it, in the same way he had sung the hymns of the Church.

Love is very patient and kind, never jealous or envious, never boastful or proud, never haughty or selfish or rude. Love does not demand its own way. It is not irritable or touchy. It does not hold grudges and will hardly even notice when others do it wrong.

It is never glad about injustice, but rejoices whenever truth wins out. If you love someone you will be loyal to him no matter what the cost. You will always believe in him, and always stand your ground in defending him.

After reading this Jim said, "This is what Jesus was like and He said that this was the nature of God, that God is Love." This is the kind of love Jim had for his daughter, but he didn't understand that, neither did the Minister of Music, or the others in the church. It is the kind of love that would have done what was right, and that is what Jim had done, he thought, when no one would trust him. Jim had disclosed himself to T. W. to try to stop what appeared to be happening to his daughter and himself. He sacrificed his feelings for her, for her own best interest. No one but Angela and Jim would know how this heartbreaking scenario had taken place.

The members sat in silence and the bell rang for them to leave. They stood, and prayer was given for them by one of the members. Jim loved all of these men. He hoped they realized that, T. W. included.

Chapter Thirteen

For several years Jim had thought of translating two of his creative pieces, To Israel and To Jerusalem into Hebrew. They were written to be translated as Hebrew poetry. He had never studied Hebrew and could not do this himself. He had read the book, "Secrets from the Lost Bible", by Dr. Kenneth Hanson, a man knowledgeable in Hebrew and thought he might communicate with him to see if he would translate for him. One of the pieces had been written spontaneously with very little editing. Jim's wife's birthday was approaching, and he had decided to purchase a card for her and give her money in it. She always liked to get money to buy supplies for her quilting activities. He had planned to get a card one Friday morning before going to the hospital to work. On the way to work, he realized that he had forgotten to get the card. He had plenty of time to stop and get a card before going in to work. Emerald Coast Mall is just across the street from Bayview Memorial where he works, so he decided to pick up a card at one of the book stores in the mall. Jim had been thinking about getting the material ready to send to Dr. Hanson concerning the translation of his creative work into Hebrew as he drove to work that day. He parked his truck outside the mall and entered the main entrance. Jim knew a book store was down two corridors on the left somewhere. He had not been in this mall in years. As he walked down the main corridor of the mall, a young lady stepped forward and stopped him, to sell some Dead Sea salt preparation. Jim said he was in a hurry. He was on his way to work and was looking to purchase a birthday card. She looked as though she was from the Middle East and he asked her if she was. She said she was from Israel. Jim went on to the bookstore and purchased the card. He couldn't get this out of his mind. He had just met a young lady from Israel. As he came back the same way he went in, he saw her there at her booth and stopped to find out more about her. "Hi." Jim said, "I'm back again. You said a moment ago, when I first came by, you were from Israel. What part of Israel are you from?" "What do you mean by that exactly?" She asked. "Oh, like what town or city do you live in?" Jim said. "Yes, I see. I am from Jerusalem. I live in Jerusalem." "You mean I am actually talking to someone who lives in Jerusalem!" Jim exclaimed. "Yes." She said. "I am from Jerusalem." "Do you know, I was looking just lately to find someone who knew Hebrew, someone who could translate two of my writings into Hebrew." "I know Hebrew." She replied. "I can translate them into Hebrew. I may have to look over them to get the feeling of what you are saying. I will be going back to Jerusalem soon. I could work on them there. I have friends who could help me." "You will take them back to Jerusalem and share them with others?" Jim asked. "Sure.—I would be happy to do this." She said. "I will bring copies of the writings to you. You can have them." Jim said spontaneously. "You will really take them back with you?" He asked. "Yes." She said. "I am happy to do so." "I can't believe this." Jim said. "I had been thinking about the translation even as I was walking through the corridor. You stepped up and stopped me. You are from Israel. You are from Jerusalem. You know Hebrew. You will translate them. You will take them back to Jerusalem! This is amazing! I can't believe it. Surely, it must be just coincidence." She interrupted pointedly. "Nothing is coincidence." She said. They shared a brief moment of wonder. They were total strangers. They didn't even know each other's names. She had no knowledge of what the writings were about. They had become friends so quickly, and it was as if they knew each other. Inside Jim was deeply moved. He began to wonder to himself. "One of the pieces has the title, 'To Jerusalem'."

Several days later Jim came back to her display in the mall. He gave her the first writing, "To Jerusalem", in a sealed manila envelope. He had added monologue which had originally accompanied it to accentuate its message. The essence of the monologue had actually unfolded from deep spiritual reflection. They had some conversation about what had happened. She reassured Jim she was pleased about this and wanted to do it.

When Jim left the display he walked down a corridor to the right, to the end, to go to the restroom. As he came back through the corridor, he stopped at an Art Gallery and was admiring the beautiful oil paintings on display. The attendant came up, and they began to discuss the pieces and his interest in art. Jim explained to her he had some old pieces he had done years ago but had not tried anything in over forty-four years, except to draw colored chalk pictures on his classroom chalk board for his students at Christmas and other occasions. The attendant then asked Jim if he would like to model for the artist. He would receive a twenty-five dollar gift certificate with no obligation to buy the portrait. The portraits were three hundred and seventy-five dollars each. Jim had never experienced anything like that before so he agreed to do it. They made an appointment for a Wednesday morning at ten o'clock. The artist was an accomplished artist of the Lakeshore area.

Jim returned promptly on the assigned day of the painting and awaited her arrival. She was a short lady with dark hair and a pleasing smile, probably about his age. They had a pleasing conversation about her work and Jim's interest in art. He mentioned the pieces he had done years ago, and she said she would like to see them. Jim said he would bring them in one day for her to see. She said she would show him some of the techniques she used in doing the work. She did, as she painted the picture in oil. Jim was greatly impressed with her skill and could sense the depth of her character. Jim knew he was a lucky man to have had this opportunity. After the work was finished and Jim had returned home, he decided to write an account of the sitting for her as a return of her favor. The sitting was videotaped for teaching purposes. Two very creative elements were present; the artist with her accomplished skill, and the musician who composed the moving piece that was used as background music. Jim hoped to add a third, a creatively written description of the event as a gift for her.

About a week later, Jim dropped by the shop to leave the pieces of art. The artist, Tina Ford, was not there at the time. The attendant was there, and as they discussed the experience, Jim related, "I also have a creative piece I have written for Tina. I was going to give it to her along with the art pieces but she is not here. It is about the sitting. You were here that day. Would you like to read it?" "Yes, I would very much like to read what you have written." I gave her the copy of the writing and she began to read it to herself....

Modeling for Tina Ford

A Moment's Pose

She set my pose.

I sat upon a stool and gazed across the mall corridor at a beautiful lady in the window of a shop.

"Who is this man?" She must have thought, "What can I see of him in the expressions of his face?"

My mind was empty at First, months and years of emotional heartbreak had dimmed the light in my soul.

"This man is interested in my life, my work, my talent and my art." She may have thought. "I will let him see a little of my work. I will give him a little of myself."

I glanced for a moment into her eyes, perhaps to see a glimpse of her inner self.

"Look past me." She said, "or I will lose my concentration."

I knew my will was strong and my soul was filled with grand visions of hope, they had always been there. I reached down for her, to bring them out of the abyss into which they had fallen.

She measured with a squint of the eye and a mark of the rod and began to set my dimensions upon the canvas.

I anchored my pose with the tri-focal of my glasses against the face of the lady in the window across the way.

What a pleasing young lady with a bright smile and the freshness and boldness of youth.

Surprisingly, she removed the canvas and turned it toward me. "This is not you yet." She said, "Just the shape upon which I will try to capture your features."

No, I thought, It is not me yet, just the general form as she said, and I am not what I really am yet, but there is still time.

Back to work she went with a wide brush. I could see some of the stroke of the brush, but not its effect. It was hidden from my view. I was beginning to relax with the beauty and smile of the young lady. I contemplated the need of my life in her, and how I had missed so many times. I had so much to give, so much, and I wanted to so much.

She was more relaxed and not so intent as she built the foundation upon which the image would form. She removed the canvas and turned it toward me. "This is still not you." she said, and explained how she had laid down the underlying base shades upon which she would catch my essence.

It was about then that music began playing in the background. I began to find myself in the moving and wistful andante of the powerful base tempo. My visions moved out over the great expanse of the Gulf of Mexico as the basses moved powerful thunderstorms across the horizon. I watched the gulls sail along the melodies as they played in the foreground of the basses and storms.

"Now", she said, "I will use the small brush to capture your features and your feeling with the oil". I saw the concentration and intent to features and expression. I saw her squint to remove bothersome detail and unveil the essence below. She would find me with her oil.

From the expanse of the horizon, the music moved the ocean waves toward the shore where they crashed upon the beach sending up a misty spray. The cellos and bases drew up a darkened cloud and from the pounding waves I heard a beloved man cry out, "You will answer to God for this!" My soul shuddered as waves crashed over me. "Oh, lift me, Holy God!" I cried!

The lady's smiling countenance moved within the mist and crying birds, as earth's life force pounded out a will, a desire, a Holy hope within me, one that had always been there.

I saw her start to make a stroke, I thought, but stopped. "It is you", she said. I watched her scrape up the formless oil from which the visions of her soul had made my likeness. I saw a man outside the shop look at me and nod with a smile of approval. I moved down from the stool and turned to look. I knew for a moment in time I had found myself again. And lo—she had baptized me with her oil.

As she finished reading the piece, she handed it back to Jim. Jim asked, "What did you think? Did you like it? She replied, "I remember the sitting. It was videotaped as it happened. I remember the comments you and Tina made and what she said is exactly as you have rendered it. Usually the music generates a bright and happy scene, but yours was a very deep and moving one. It made me want to cry." "I appreciate your comments. They are very important to me. Would you please give Tina this writing and the drawings and tell her I said they are hers to keep. I will probably be back by sometime later to talk to her about them." "Sure I will." She said. "I know she will be very happy to have them."

After leaving the art gallery, Jim stopped back by the Dead Sea Salt shop to talk to Sarit Yishai (The name of the young Jewish lady). He asked her if she was offended by anything in the writing. Jim also mentioned that he was a Christian, but not an ordinary one. He was not trying to convert Jews to Christian doctrine. He was just giving his heart to the people of Jerusalem and to the world for that matter. Sarit said she was not offended, she thought he was a very good writer. She was excited about this and very much wanted to do it. Jim met her husband, and they talked about Israel. He also said Sarit would do this, she would take his writing back to Israel. Jim was pleased at what she had said. He had not offended her with the writing, and she really seemed to want to do this. He knew nothing about her. She was a complete stranger. Somehow or other he felt this was destined to happen. Only time would indicate its purpose, if any.

Jim returned to the mall about a week later. The art shop had moved up to the front of the mall where it would be more visible. He stopped in, and Tina was there. They had a delightful conversation. She said she had written Jim a letter and was going to mail it, but since he was there she gave it to him then. She suggested he should try to publish the piece in one of the music journals. Jim said the piece was hers. He had given it to her, and she could use it in any way she desired. The letter Tina gave him was written inside a card with a portrait on the front, in oil on canvas, of Tina Ford's daughter-in-law. Jim knew he would keep it as memory of a great lady and a great experience.

Jim also visited the display where Sarit worked. He carried the other piece in a sealed manila envelope and gave it to her. The title of the piece was, "To Israel". He knew this one had more of a Christian slant and hoped she would not misunderstand his intentions. They had a long conversation about Israel and about his love for her people and Jerusalem. Jim reiterated the fact that he was not trying to convert Jews to the doctrines of Christianity some of which were questionable in his own mind. He spoke to her about her name. "Your name, Sarit Yihsai, what does it mean in your language?" "Oh my first name, It is the same as Abraham's wife, Sarah in English. My last name is the name of the house of David." She said. "Do you mean Jessie the English one given in the Bible?" "Yes that is the one I mean. It is the Hebrew name as your Jessie in the Bible." Again, in the silence of his mind, Jim was flabbergasted. He remembered the dream he had, how Angela had slept at his feet as Ruth had at Boaz's. How the presence of the essence of the Spirit had become imminently recognizable to him, and a peace he had never experienced before swept over him. In the Bible, Ruth and Boaz were the grandparents of David the King, of the house of Jesse (Yishai). Jim knew, if no one else did, he and Angela's relationship was physical and emotional but also deeply spiritual and, he felt, had a holy purpose. It would be for time and the hand of the Spirit to reveal it. "Could this be a part of it"? He asked himself. His mind was filled with wonder. Jim bought some Dead Sea salt preparation from her, but he had to demand payment for it. She took only her cost for it. Jim knew he would also keep this as a memory of an extraordinary experience.

The next time Jim went by Sarit's display Sarit had left that very day for Israel. One of the other gentlemen there said she would be in New York at the present time waiting for her plane to depart, and Jim could call her on his cell phone if he should like to. Jim said he wouldn't bother her now. The man said her husband was over at the other display and he could talk to him if he liked. Jim walked over to her husband's display and spoke to him. He assured

Jim that she had his writings and was taking them to Israel with her. Jim said Sarit promised to e-mail him the translations and he asked him to remind her, if he would.

Regardless of the outcome, these events have been a wonder to Jim. Had He not come there by chance that day, He would not have met Sarit. Surely, he would not have had his portrait rendered by Tina Ford. He would not have obtained much emotional release by sharing some of his personal life with others.

Jim went to church again after a week or two of being absent. Angela was there in the choir. Jim was glancing at Angela, he could not stop himself, and she was also looking at him. He noticed Dorothy, who was sitting beside him to his left, turn and look at him. When she did not turn away, Jim looked around at her. Dorothy was scowling at him. Jim looked up at Angela and Angela was almost laughing at them. When Dorothy turned her head away, Jim looked at Angela and laughingly smiled at her. "What, in heaven's name, is all of this about?" Jim thought. How is it, that two people can be so in sync and yet never have a face to face conversation to clear up any of it one way or the other?

Jim had noticed earlier that people knowledgeable about this situation had been stationed in strategic places to keep anything serious from happening between him and the men involved, or perhaps, as a protection for Angela, as if one was needed. Jim would let them know, when he realized this, He knew what was happening. One time Jim commented laughingly to the Administrative Assistant, "Got the guard duty tonight, Huh?" Jim could tell he was right about what he was doing there. The picture was clear to Jim now. T. W. was pressing to have him disciplined for adultery and was trying to have him pegged as pursuing or even stalking his daughter. It is possible she may have made a complaint such as this in defense of her untenable situation. T. W. was telling people Jim had a problem and he didn't want his daughter around him. Jim really didn't know what Angela's role was in this, but he knew he had left it open for her to protect herself and her social status. Jim was never critical of her in any way. He wanted it that way. Angela knew in her heart what had happened to her, and what she had tried to do. She would have to live with it just as Jim would. T. W. was reacting to protect his daughter to "save face" for her and didn't really know that Jim had acted in every way for her own best interest also. After the scowling event Jim was informed by Dorothy that she was not going back to that Church any more. "All you want to do is sit there and stare at Angela. I am not going back after what Ted did, and if you do you may as well get a divorce." Ted, the official that had met with Mark and Jim, had testified in court against the daughter of one of Dorothy's friends.

The next Wednesday night Jim learned that Mark Davis' grandmother had died. Angela was not there. Jim thought she might be with her husband at the funeral home. In the message Brother Steve had mentioned how some were facing divorce and new beginnings and how David had been forgiven of his sin with Bathsheba. You can bet that Jim wondered what he was talking about. Were Angela and Mark separating because of all that had happened between him and Angela? After the prayer meeting, Jim was surprised to see her come in. Jim was over in the left isle. T. W. was in the center aisle. Angela came up and began talking to her dad. Jim walked out into the vestibule. He waited, hoping he would get a chance to talk to them. It was then that one of the leaders of the church came up to him and started a conversation. He mentioned that he had talked to some of his female coworkers at Bayview Memorial Hospital when he was there visiting the sick. He said they had spoken quite highly of him and he was delighted. He had known Jim since high school days, and they were good friends. He said that in all of his years he had never heard anyone say anything bad about Jim. It was always good. Jim told him he didn't think he had talked to everybody. They laughed about that. He could tell that Jim was watching Angela. Jim really wanted to talk to her and her dad. What could happen with her dad there? He was willing to try one last time to mend this schism between Jim's family and his. His friend just kept talking, intentionally it seemed, and would not let Jim get near her. They talked for over thirty minutes. The choir was already in session, and they were singing practice songs. Everyone else had left. Finally they closed their conversation and said goodbye. His friend left out the main entrance of the church. Jim walked over to the open door at the back of the sanctuary and stood in the opening. He looked out across the church at the choir. He wanted so much to sing in this choir. He and Angela could have sung the songs of the church together. What a joy that would have been. They were singing a song. Angela was there singing. She was watching the director lead the practice. She would not turn and look. Jim stood there for what seemed an eternity. She knew he was there. Everyone else in the choir also knew he was standing there. Jim was saying goodbye. Goodbye to her and goodbye to the church. Goodbye to the choir, goodbye to the congregation, and goodbye to the people Jim loved so much. He knew he would never be able to worship there with this situation unresolved. He didn't know what was happening between her and her husband. It was her turn now. If he ever knew the intent of her heart, she would have to reveal it to him. There had been so much heartbreak, so many good intentions shattered, so much possibility for good lost. Jim still didn't know what was in the heart of this beautiful lady. It was not just the passion, she was connected to everything dear it seemed, everything holy in his life.

Chapter Fourteen

W hen Jim got home after saying goodbye to everyone in his heart that night, Dorothy said she had received an e-mail through her computer web-site from a Mister McDowell. He wanted to know if Jim would like to meet an Anita Hays. Jim asked Dorothy if he was one of the McDowells from church. Dorothy said she had asked him and he had said no, he wasn't one of them. At the moment Jim's mind was focused on possible students he had taught at school. Jim had taught several Hays students, both boys and girls. He could not remember on the spur of the moment a student by the name of Anita Hays. Jim asked Dorothy why he would ask her such a question, why didn't he ask him. Dorothy was at a loss as to why he had sent her the e-mail. Jim told Dorothy he didn't have an interest in meeting anyone named Anita Hays and to relate that message to him. He didn't know a student by that name if that was what the inquiry was about. Later as Jim pondered what this meant in light of all of the things that were happening at this time, it dawned on him what it might be about. Years ago before he had ever dated Dorothy when he was teaching aviation ground school, he had met a girl named Ava Grice. She had enrolled in one of his ground school classes. Ava's father was an airline pilot and through conversation about this and the ground school class, Ava and Jim had become friends. She was a rather tall young woman with dark eyes and black hair. Ava was a real good looker in her own way and was a wild and crazy woman to put it mildly. She explained to Jim once how she used to roller skate through the malls. They dated a few times. She was really fun to be with, and Jim liked her a lot. He took her flying several times. He would do all of the crazy aerobatic maneuvers and simulated crop dusting of the farm fields, and she would just be exhilarated and want more. She loved flying and had every confidence in Jim and his old J3. Jim really appreciated that and he liked her a lot, but Betsy Lee was the person on his mind at the time. Jim mentioned Betsy Lee to her and the difficulty he was having. Her only comment to him about it was, "Go for it!" even though Jim had said she was married. She was that kind of girl. Ava had related a lot to Jim about her dad. Jim had come to know a little about what he did for entertainment and what kind of car he drove. One night Jim drove out to one of the bars that Ava had mentioned he frequented. His car was there. Jim had never met him and didn't know what he looked like. As Jim walked in he scanned the room to see if he might recognize him. Knowing what he knew about him, he saw the only one in the room that he could be, sitting on a bar stool at the bar. Jim pulled up a bar stool next to him and ordered a beer. They began a conversation that people at bars are good at. They had not introduced themselves. After about ten minutes Jim looked at him and said, "You must be an airline pilot." He looked a little startled, collected himself, and said, "Yes I am, and you must be a ground school instructor!" He had quickly realized Jim was Ava's ground school instructor. They carried on a lively conversation after that for over an hour. That was when two ladies came in and were seated. He recognized them and asked Jim to join him with them. Jim did and through the night they socialized and danced together there in the bar. Ava's dad had paired with the older lady, and Jim had become friends with the younger girl. When it came time to leave, Ava's dad said he was going to go home with the girls and Jim had may as well come along with them. Jim did, and Jim and the girl became close friends after that. They met several times, and she went flying with him on one occasion. Jim carried her home to a relative's house on Memorial Drive after one date. She said she was from Arkansas and was visiting relatives. After a date one night, the conversation came around to birth control medication. She said she was not taking any birth control medication. Jim was shocked and somewhat stunned. As this unfolded, Jim had expected her to be taking birth control medication. He stopped seeing her after this. Of course this had ended the relationship he had with Ava. The girl's name was Anita Hays. After this recollection Jim related it to Dorothy and explained how this might be the reason the person e-mailed her about it. Possibly to embarrass him in front of her amid all of the things that was happening. Dorothy accepted it for what it was without questioning because she knew both of them had a life of their own before they married.

Jim was in the grocery store one day after this and met T. W.'s daughter in-law. He apologized to her for anything he might have done to hurt anyone in their family. They had always been friends. She was a member of the medical profession. She said she did not believe that Jim had hurt anyone she knew of. He asked her how T. W. was. She said he was doing fine. He was taking a trip to visit an old friend in Arkansas. When she said Arkansas, it dawned on Jim then, with this connection, an explanation for some of the wild and crazy things that had happened to him. One of the ministers at Cedar Hill Baptist Church back at the time he was teaching ground school was a man named Hays. Jim had never thought of this until now. T. W. had been a member of Cedar Hill Baptist Church before he and others had formed Lakeview Baptist Church years ago. He was a very close friend of Preacher Hays. At the time, Preacher Hays lived close to Memorial Drive. Jim wondered if there might be a connection between himself, Anita Hays's grandchildren, if she had any, and Angela Davis' children. Jim knew nothing about Angela's children. He knew the two younger daughters did not favor the older girl. He wondered if they were Angela's natural children or were they adopted. If there was a connection, it could explain a lot of things. It might explain Angela's unusual behavior, especially the events concerning her children. It could explain the incident at Arby's. It might explain her lack of communication and the depth and persistence of her emotional engagement. It could have been the reason Jim was directed to have no contact with her children, and why her father had questioned his character. It would explain the e-mail that Dorothy had received from Mr. McDowell. What was the real story in the mind of this Angel? Was there really a connection between Jim and one of her children? Was it possible that one of Angela's children was thought to be his grandchild? Jim marveled now at the possibility. Boaz was a kinsman redeemer. Did she have a vision, or a dream, that involved him, as he had of her? Jim really thought she had. He could remember comments made by Brother Steve when this was beginning. One was, "A person was willing to give up everything for what *she* thought God was asking *her* to do." This was made in such a way as to exonerate the person he was talking about by innuendo. Jim thought he was talking about Angela. Imagination or not, this was one thing that made him falter, was the Holy Spirit really leading them in this way? How could this possibly be true? Christians are taught that the Spirit does not call people to hurt others or to violate the established moral and secular laws. In the same emotion-filled delivery Brother Steve was directing his comments to Angela's mom and dad by his non verbal contact, when he said, "God does not call a person to leave their own family and marry someone else." In a charge to the congregation to, "forget about it." "Just forget about it", (whatever that meant) possibly talk about Angela and Jim, the preacher had said outright, "He is not hers and she is not his." Jim believed many people knew they had an emotional relationship with each other in an impossible scenario. Jim feared most people thought it was his doing, his intent. It had to be obvious at the peak of their interaction. Some wept for them. Some prayed for them. Jim's mind was filled simultaneously with joy and grief. Yet, he could see himself being seen by others as an interloper or a Satan with the power to mesmerize a young woman with sensual desire. He knew, also, that some of this could be his own imagination. Jim suffered at his own rejection of her *supposed* willingness to sacrifice everything to marry him. Jim had no idea at the time about any possible connection between him and her children. All of this had taken place without a word, a single word about it passing between them except, "I'm going to bring you a bunch of angels." What was in her mind that day when she said this in front of people who could hear? Jim probably will never know. It was as if the hand of

God was directing this heartbreaking tragedy, as if somewhere in a future time the reason for it all would be known, and great things would happen because of it.

Dorothy and Jim did not go back to Lakeview Church any more after that. Jim debated in his own mind just what he would do concerning church. He did try to keep up with Angela's whereabouts, but he could no longer risk making any contact with her himself. Jim knew she could contact him easily if she wanted to. Jim believed that one day he would get some kind of message from her, to explain her point of view and relieve some of the emotional stress that both of them had undergone. Jim thought Brother Steve was sure they were having a full-blown affair. Jim really thought he expected them to eventually divorce and remarry unless there was some other scenario Angela was anticipating. Brother Steve did not know this was not the case. Jim had never touched this person or ever tried to make any advance toward her other than the nonverbal, emotional contact they had that she had originally experienced when they were at church together. Jim had no intentions of destroying her marriage. He had made this clear to her father and this, Jim thought, was what precipitated the confrontation. He probably persuaded Angela that Jim would never marry her when Jim sent her the last e-mail. T. W. may have felt Jim had led her on until she became emotionally involved with him and then would not follow through, either physically or through commitment. If T. W. did think the relation between her children and Jim was true, whether Jim knew or not was always a question in his mind and he may have believed that Jim knew about it and would not act. T. W.'s question: "What makes you think Angela has any interest in you?" may have been an attempt to find out, and Jim's innocent answer: "There are things you can't know." May have led him to believe Jim did know. Jim knew his fatherhood of a child of Anita Hays had never been officially and objectively established. No discussions ever took place between Anita Hays and him concerning a child. Jim was questioned once by a third party who had some knowledge of the situation but Jim never heard anything from Anita Hays again, and he never thought about it again until the question from Mr. Mc Dowell, and the incident with T.W.'s daughter in law helped him make the possible connection to Angela Davis's children. Heartbreakingly, Jim remembered a preacher from times back admonishing everyone, "Rest assured, your sins will find you out."

Angela had cut her hair and had it curled the next time Jim saw her, (from a distance) and his heart sank because he knew she was going through some difficult times. Jim could not contact her under the circumstances. She would have to contact him if any contact was made at all. It was really difficult for Jim those first few weeks and months not knowing anything and not having any communication with anyone about the situation. Even those he had conversation with that he knew and could trust would indicate they knew nothing about this situation. They knew nothing about her personal life or whether she and her husband had separated. When school let out and she was free from work, Jim thought surely she would try to contact him in some way. This never happened. Jim began to try to see what she was doing and where she was going. Late one night when he returned from work at Bayview Memorial, he passed by her house on the road where she lived and noticed that her car was not there. A grey car had been there off and on since he left the church, but he wasn't real sure it was her husband's. It could have been her older daughter's. Jim made a loop around by the church and out County Road Nine to Johnson road. If she was in Lakeshore she would be coming back from that direction. Sure enough, Jim had not gone far up Johnson Road when he met the red sport utility vehicle, and tail-gaiting right behind it was a smaller red car. Jim made a turn around and went back down the road where she lived. The red utility vehicle and the small red car were parked in her garage and all of the lights were on. Of course it could have been one of her girl friends from her school or the church. Many of them had red cars.

Dorothy and Jim had not been attending church anywhere and one Sunday morning during the time of the last service at Lakeview Church, Jim went to Winn Dixie to get some lunch for Dorothy, Joseph and himself. As he walked up to the entrance he saw one of her daughters walk by in front of him. He looked to his left toward the parking lot and saw Angela a short distance away pushing a shopping cart toward the parking lot. Jim called out to her twice, and he knew she heard him, but she just kept going toward her car. Jim stopped there and watched until she reached her car. Then he thought, "What am I doing standing here?", and followed her out to her car where she was loading up the groceries. It was not her red SUV. It was one of the small grey cars that he had seen parked at her home. She did not see him coming and Jim did not want to startle her, so he called out to her just before he reached her. She looked up at him and acknowledged him but did not say anything. One of her daughters was standing by the open car door facing Jim. She was smiling and seemed glad to see him there. As always the apprehension mounted to the freezing point, and all Jim could muster was, "Angela. Are you ok?" "Yes, I am fine", she replied, and kept unloading groceries. Though they made eye contact and there was acceptance, all Jim could see was a burden of stress and a kind of disappointing resolution. He never knew for sure if she was trying to leave her husband to marry him. Jim could not think clearly enough to start the right conversation that would reveal the many things he so desperately needed to know. She saw him look at her hair with a definite air of despair and sadness, and she just looked off and kept unloading. Jim managed a "How is your dad?" She said, "Oh, he is ok. He stays in that garden all of the time." And then for the first time she instigated an inquiry, and she really looked concerned. "Are *you* doing ok?" With his heart saddened he said, "Yes I am ok, I am ok." Immediately he recognized the same line he had given before and knew he should have said, "No, Angela, I am not ok, I am not ok—let's talk." but he didn't. She seemed somewhat relieved when he said he was ok, almost as if Jim was accepting what had happened, and releasing her of any obligation toward him. Then Jim said, "Well I just wanted to come and say hello." At that Jim turned and left, knowing he had missed a chance to relieve a lot of grief and suffering. Jim had said he was ok before, and she knew he was not ok. Maybe she would remember that and know he needed to talk openly to her. It was not that Jim wanted her to embrace him but for her to reveal her intentions and feelings, for her to openly disclosed to him what had happened to them and why from her perspective. Was there really a connection between him and her children? What was the secret happening or consequence that caused her to pursue him so strongly, to the point of breaking his marriage, that she could not reveal to him? Maybe some other time, some other day they would be able to talk openly and honestly to one another.

One Wednesday night after the church had dismissed prayer meeting, Jim drove down the road where Angela lived on his way to Wal-Mart and met two cars coming down the road. He just glimpsed the person in the first car, a grey car, and it looked like Angela with her curled hair. The next car was obviously following closely. When it passed it was a small red car and the person inside looked like his divorced cousin, Bill Jernigan, also a member of Lakeview Church. This startled Jim, but things began to become a little clearer now. Bill had previously dated Cathy Nixon, a friend of Angela's. Jim knew Angela hung out with Cathy. If Angela was having any trouble at home and was stepping out on her husband he would have had an opportunity to get involved. Jim knew Bill quit dating Cathy. He was extremely bothered by all of this, but he kept his distance.

Jim went to a birthday celebration for one of his relatives shortly after this. It was a great time. Once again Jim was making contact with many of the people he loved, and they were accepting him openly and without question. Dorothy was there with him. Bill Jernigan was also there. Jim noticed that Bill seemed to be avoiding any contact with him. He had removed himself to another room where some children were playing basketball. Jim walked over into the room and greeted him. He mentioned he wanted to talk to him sometime. Bill said they could go into another room and talk. Jim said no, he would come by his home one day and talk to him. Jim went by his home shortly after that, and he was cooking outside for his children and some of his children's guests. They sat down at a table, and Jim began to divulge some of the things that had happened between Angela and him. Jim explained what he could not do about the situation and said, "You know me well enough to know I could not do that." Bill said, "No, I know you could not do something like that." Bill seemed to be good friends with her husband. Jim had seen him a lot with Mark at church. Jim thought maybe he would have some answers. He began to ask him personal questions about Angela. Jim asked Bill if he knew anything about her personal life and whether she and her husband had ever had trouble at home. He asked if she and her husband were presently together. Bill denied knowing anything about Angela or her personal life. He denied having any contact with her. He did mention that he thought Angela and her husband were having trouble at one time. Jim noticed he was very self-conscious during his questioning and really projected some self-consternation. Bill had always loved Jim. Jim had known him as a child and Bill's father loved Jim and Jim loved him. He had lost his father to a heart attack many years ago. When Jim started to leave Bill said to him. "Time will heal it. Time will take care of it. Just go on from here and let everything work its self out." Jim cautioned him to take care and be careful. The be careful projected a thought that Bill might know more about this that he could bring himself to tell him, knowing that he loved him.

Shortly after this Jim was admitted to the hospital with angina pectoris, a condition his father and several of his father's brothers had experienced. Jim required a heart catheterization and had two stints placed into his heart. This required two separate admissions to the hospital. One thing saddened Jim about this. Not a single person from the church, including Brother Jim, contacted him or visited him during his two admissions to the hospital. What was this infuriated and incensed father telling everyone about him? It appeared that committing outright adultery would have been easier on him. What was this seemingly rejected lady and embarrassed husband communicating to others about him? Jim could guess, and this caused him quite a bit of frustration and worry. Jim had never spoken to anyone in the church in his defense other than the generalizations he had given in his meeting with Mark Davis. Jim tried hard to protect Angela. One reason he did was because he loved T. W. and Jacqueline so much. Jim began to wonder if it was worth it. Jim wrote a letter to one of his cousins who is directly connected to this family. Jim had visited him personally and asked his permission to write it in order to make a record. It outlined the way things had unfolded and Jim's intentions but did not get overly specific. Jim wanted him to know the truth from his perspective because he had always been a very close family member. Jim didn't know what they might have told him.

Jim became removed from any knowledge or activities about this situation as he recovered from the heart surgery. As time passed on it became obvious that Angela did not want to have any communication with Jim, that is, communication that she would instigate. One day Jim drove down Cypress Street on his way to Winn Dixie. It passes within a few feet of the school where Angela teaches. Jim didn't know which room was hers, but as he drove by, Jim glanced through the open windows and doors. As he looked through one door, he saw her seated at her desk teaching her children. She was looking out her door as he passed and they saw each other again, if only a glance. For the briefest moment the contact that they always had was vaguely rekindled. Jim had not meant for this to happen, he was just driving by. A week or so later, he passed by the school again. When he came to her door, a curtain had been installed, and it was drawn over the door, closing off any view from the outside. Jim knew then in an ever so subtle way that she had broken any possible relationship with him. Jim knew this was best, but he could not shut out the overwhelming remorse and sadness. Not that he had lost the favor of this beautiful and intelligent young lady, but that he had lost a beautiful relationship with her, her father, and all of her family. Yes, it had become a tragedy indeed. A tragedy for Jim and a tragedy for Angela and it need not have been in any way whatsoever. Jim wondered to himself, "Will I ever know what was in the heart of this lady?"

Chapter Fifteen

As always, when the need came for Jim to sort out things and clear the air of all of the frustration and anxiety, he would take a ride through the country of his heart. Jim always loved his Uncle Oliver with the deepest love. He had spent so much of his time nurturing him and guiding him in life. He was always there. He didn't work as many days per week as his father, so he had more free time to do things. He never left Jim out of the things he enjoyed. He would pick him up after school just to go bird hunting a few hours in the afternoon. His Uncle Oliver drove the country roads of North Florida and Southern Alabama to buy chickens which he sold to dressing companies in Lakeshore, Florida. Jim would go with him often, helping catch and load chickens. Uncle Oliver had helped Jim learn to drive on these old roads, and he drove for him often. The trips were always more than just work though. They would visit with people he knew in the small hamlets and towns and just have a great time getting to know others. They would eat in the special little country cafes he had located and have a great time talking with the owners and patrons. Uncle Oliver always treated Jim with the highest regard in their company. To him Jim was something special. One can see what this would do for the self esteem of a young boy. Can you imagine how Jim would suffer if he thought in any way he had let him down, that he had not met the expectations his Uncle Oliver had of him? They were the highest one could imagine because he and all of his family were just great people. They weren't as much what he expected Jim to accomplish as who he expected Jim to be as a person. They were the Christian values of behavior, though he was not a church member and never preached to him one word. Uncle

Oliver lived his values he did not preach them. All of Jim's family was like this, including his father. They were really great people. Jim could always find relief and joy riding the country roads and visiting the small hamlets and towns. This was what he needed to do now, to take a trip, to take a look at life again.

Jim came up Highway Twenty-Nine bypass from Lakeshore, after taking care of some business, and turned left on Court Street where he lives. He lives on the North corner there so he turned right at the first driveway by his mailbox. He has five acres of land here with a huge frontage on both Highway Twenty-Nine and Court Street. The Court Street frontage runs for some distance all the way to the next cleared lot and house. After securing everything at home, Jim left again going North on Highway Twenty-Nine. He wanted to drive through some of the country he and his Uncle had frequented so long ago. He turned east, traveled for some distance, and intersected Florida State Highway Eighty-Seven at the Berrydale Crossroads. Jim stopped at the Berrydale Crossroads Citgo station on the right and filled his gas tank. He also bought some chicken livers and a diet coke to munch on as he traveled on North toward Brewton, Alabama. Not long after the Berrydale Crossroads he passed through Fidelis where the Rowells, have property. Keith Rowell and others play and sing on Friday nights in the old Fidelis School long since closed. About halfway between Fidelis and Dixonville, Jim passed by T. D. and Cassie Jamieson's old home place. It sits up on a small hill right on the road. Jim, his Dad, and Uncle Oliver, would visit T. D. and go quail hunting in the area around his house. Jim loved those people, and he knew why. His mother and father, Aunt Sarah and Uncle Oliver loved them dearly, and T. D. and Cassie loved all of them too. Of course, Jim enjoyed the male camaraderie with T. D, his Dad and Uncle Oliver. They were all good quail shots and had good dogs. As Jim passed by he thought about the good times with them and wondered why he had not bought that house when it went on the market. He came here one summer day a few years ago before the home was purchased. The old pear tree was loaded down with sumptuous fruit. Many were lying all over the ground under the tree. He picked up a few, munched on a few and knew T. J. and Cassie would have said, "Eat all you want, son, what's ours is yours and these are ours." T. J. and Cassie have long since passed away as have all of Jim's older relatives except his sister Mary. T. J. and Cassie's one daughter, Peggy, lives in Fort Walton and is a writer. This was a beautiful place long ago, with rolling hills, huge tall pines and little underbrush. What made it really beautiful to Jim though was the friendship and love of the people who lived there. The old site has been raped, as so much land has been, since the paper companies arrived. It is clear cut, almost barren and eroding. The view is a perfect picture of a part of Jim's heart in that respect. "Where is the love and trust families should have with one another *these* days?" Jim thought. Jim wanted Angela's whole family to trust him and love him, to know that his love was pure and righteous and that he would never violate his or her troth. But a savage selfish wind had come and violated his trust and blew his good intentions away, clear away as the clear cut land that lay devastated before him.

Jim passed on by as life passes on by. On up the old road he traveled, as he had so many times with his Uncle Oliver. The sky was a clear blue, the air cool and fresh with a vague hint of spring not too far away. Jim regained the exuberance, hope and joy he had always possessed as he witnessed the beautiful scenery pass by on the old road. He passed by the Camp Henderson road as he approached Dixonville and the Alabama State Line at the Old Travis Road. As he left Dixonville he could see the Navy flight trainers making their touch and go approaches to Brewton Airfield. Jim had landed on the end of that runway once, on a day such as this, jumping out of his old J-3 Cub while it was still running to go to the bathroom. There was no *bathroom* there of course. He rolled into Riverview just before crossing the Conecuh River and could smell the good cooking coming from the little store at the crossroads. Jim has eaten there many times. They have good old country food. He had been munching on his chicken livers and drinking diet coke so he didn't need to stop. The river was up a little as rains had relieved some of the drought in the area. Jim had flown down this river one time in his old J-3. He had flown just a few feet over the water, around the bends, over the bridges, by the fishermen in their boats, from North of McClellan where the new bridge crosses to this bridge at Brewton. Driving on, he passed by the intersection of Highway Twenty-Nine that goes to Andalusia, Alabama as he entered East Brewton. He passed Ridge Road as he approached Murder Creek, crossed over the Buddy Mitchell Bridge on Highway Forty-One and went through the lights to the light at the railroad. They have paintings on the buildings like they have in Lakeshore, Florida where he lives. One at the railroad shows old timber workers and a spur engine on rails that hauled logs to the mills. Jim loves these old paintings. He has so many memories of the stories his father and his father's brothers told about their experiences, dipping turpentine, driving logs, deadheading for logs, skidding logs out of swamps, cutting crossties for railroads such as these and, Juniper shingles for the roofs of houses and buildings. What men they were! Good men mentally and physically who knew who they were and what they were living and working for. Of course, this was for their families and the ones they loved. No doubt about it, this was their reason for living. Their role as a Southern male was clear and unquestioned as was the role of the women in their life. They would brag about how their mother would arise at four o'clock in the morning to fire up an old wood stove and cook breakfast for the nine men in their household with the help of her four daughters and one foster child. The men would have given their life for these women and they knew it. The women loved the men and loved fulfilling their part in maintaining the household. They wanted to work for them. Life was hard, but they loved life and were full of grace and love, not bickering and complaining. They found joy and happiness in meeting the needs of their families. Jim knew, even as a man, he felt this need. The need to work for the ones he loved. The need to give to the ones he really loved. It came from the men and women in his family.

Jim intended to go up the East side of Burnt Corn Creek between Highway Forty-One on the west and Highway Thirty-One on the East, so he turned right at the light onto Highway

Thirty-One and went for a block or two, where he turned left to reach Highway Forty-Nine north. This road begins as a street by office buildings and the Court House and continues through the old residential area of aristocratic Brewton, Alabama. One can't help but think of ancient Rome or Greece as one drives up this road. Huge old homes, with massive white columns, testify to the wealth and affluence of the people who had them built here. The further north one goes, the smaller the columns become, being replaced eventually with moderate homes, and finally country homes and woodland. Ah, country homes and woodland, Jim breathed a sigh of relief to be out of town. He traveled on up Forty Nine North, through the community of Appleton, until he reached a place called Sand Cut, where he turned left onto Highway Six that comes from Castleberry. He stopped at a store on the left at the intersection of Interstate Sixty-Five and got another coke to go with the last of the chicken livers. Jim talked briefly to the clerk about the weather. He was refreshed and ready to see more country. He crossed Interstate Sixty-Five and immediately angled off to the right on a road that would carry him to State Road Fifteen. On up Road Fifteen he went, through some pretty farming country and homes where the road was lined with pecan trees. Eventually Jim could see the Hampton Ridge water tank off in the distance to the North West. Finally he came to U.S. Highway Eighty-Four, east of Repton, Alabama at a place called Belleville. Jim crossed U.S. Highway Eighty-Four and continued north on Fifteen. He traveled through country primarily occupied by colored folks it seemed and recognized the same yard full of colored guys that he had seen on a previous trip up this roadway. Jim believed they recognized him. He thought about stopping but decided against it. They looked like they had nothing important to do. They may have thought he was a drug dealer or something. Later, he passed by an older man that gave a friendly wave. He seemed more like his kind of person. Jim didn't stop. He just kept going. Jim travels armed just in case. He has a nine millimeter Makarov semiautomatic pistol, in his glove compartment, and a large non-folding, sheathed, hunting knife in the pocket on the left door panel of his truck. That's where they stay until some real emergency arises. Jim has no violent tendencies but knows the risks of traveling alone and believes in being prepared. There was a strong feeling of abandonment about the area as he traveled on north on this road. It was an empty feeling as if what had made it once a bustling place with a colorful history was gone. Jim knew he hoped his truck would keep on trucking. He eventually reached the Old Stage Coach Road Five which took him toward Burnt Corn, Alabama. Jim drove Road Five a short distance to the old buildings at Burnt Corn. It was once a stagecoach stop on the old Federal Road through Indian Territory. He had the same feelings of abandonment; of being off the beaten path that haunted him earlier. Burnt Corn is an important place in the history of Jim's people. The Battle of Burnt Corn between the militia and Indians in 1813 helped precipitate a Massacre of white settlers led by the mixed blood Red Stick Creek Chief, Red Eagle, at Fort Mims on the Alabama River. One of Jim's distant grandfathers and his wife died in Fort Mims. Ironically, Jim is also a direct descendant of high ranking Indian leaders of the Cherokee, Chickasaw and Powhatan Confederacy some of which helped found the towns and cities in the area where Jim lives.

Jim can hear the conversation now. "Have you ever been to Burnt Corn, Alabama?" "Yes!" Jim said. "I went there once on some important business." "Yeah?", "What could be important in Burnt Corn?" "Well," Jim said, "It wasn't so much Burnt Corn the place but getting there. I traveled the old roads back into the past. Back into the past of unfulfilled dreams and hopes. Back with the Uncle I loved on the old roads, back to my roots where the real heart of my life had its beginnings. Back where the view was clear and not so confusing. Back where the people knew me and knew my heart. Back to the love that sustained me, and sustains me, and lets me know I have done the right thing regardless of the pain. Back where the men were tough, with character and discipline, and the women were honorable and virtuous. Back to replay the most important things in my life that gave me meaning and purpose, an important trip. Now I knew why, clearly again, I could not do the things I did not do. It was not a fault of not seizing the moment; it was not a fault of missed opportunity that I was punishing myself about. It was the strength of honor and dignity and love and righteousness I was given as gifts that was sustaining me all of the time. What was it to them that I had loved them 'With the love I seemed to lose with my lost saints and with my childhood's faith?'[2] What was it to her that I would not violate her troth? And even now, what was it to her that I would not violate my troth? I may never know. But I need not know because I know myself and what sustains me, and I can see it clearly now. "Have you ever been to Burnt Corn?" "Yes. I drove up there just lately, one bright and sunny day, as my Uncle and I had done so many years ago."

Jim left Burnt Corn and drove south down Old Stage Coach Road Five to the town of Bermuda. He laughed when he thought about it. "When Dorothy asks me where I've been, I'll say. I've been to Bermuda!" Dorothy loves him he knows, she tells him all of the time, and he loves her. Jim realizes it clearly now, their children have been a real blessing to everyone around. What gifts they have been given! He turned right onto County Road Twenty which leads to Monroeville, Alabama, a town he planned to visit on his road trip today. Jim had never traveled this road that he could remember, and as he moved on in toward Monroeville the clear blue sky and crisp clean air magnified the beauty of the farms, fields and woodlands. He intersected State Road Twenty-One as he entered Monroeville and passed through the main part of town to the light at the courthouse square. This quaint old courthouse is a famous historical site because of the Pulitzer Prize winning book "To Kill a Mockingbird" written by Harper Lee. Truman Capote also lived here in Monroeville through part of his early childhood. Jim parked his car at the curb and read all of the historical displays outside. He had spent a lot of time here the first time he visited this site, so he moved quickly into the building and through several rooms on the ground floor, enjoying the history and the building. He climbed the stairs to the courtroom above. The grand court room had a stately

2   Henry W. Longfellow, "How do I Love Thee, The Pocket Book of Verse (New York: Pocket Books, Inc, 1958, excerpts, 10-12

aura about it as his mind imagined the activities and drama that surely took place here. The lawyers and judges and their support personnel, the accused and the witnesses, the jurors and onlookers came to life in their places amid the empty court room where some dared to speak against the social injustice that lived in this small southern town. Yes, Jim thought, it lives in every town, north or south. And not just racial social injustice, social injustice of sundry forms and kinds within the struggling minds of men. The Indian peoples of old here knew much about injustice. Tradition dies hard, and some pernicious social traditions began to die here.

Jim went down another flight of stairs to the main floor below and into a large open room. He was greeted with a broad, beautiful smile and a pleasant, cheerful "Hello, can I help you, sir?" by a very pretty lady seated at a desk on one side of the room. "Oh I am just passing through, enjoying the history once again. The building and courtroom are as beautiful as their history is important." Jim said. They talked for a while, and Jim learned about her work with the Historical Society and a few things about her personal life. There was no one else in the room, and Jim noticed the palpable acceptance of his personal presence and the nonverbal attraction that was obvious to both of them. He sensed her self-awareness, as she fidgeted with the cut of her blouse in an attempt to close it some. Jim tried hard to ignore the somewhat embarrassing attraction and was as courteous and proper as he could be. He thanked her for her help and friendliness and left. Outside, Jim remembered a small buffet he had visited on his first trip. He walked around the block to the corner and saw the "Sweet Tooth Bakery" sign that adorned the front of the building of the small restaurant. As he walked up to the counter where the buffet was located, he passed a pretty young lady going to her seat with her meal. Their eyes met as they passed and Jim thought, "Oh goodness, not again." The servers were a jovial older couple, Mr. and Mrs. Lloyd Clark, and they struck up an enjoyable conversation as they served him his meal. Jim went to a seat close by where he could see everyone and look out of the window in front. He noticed the young lady sitting in the very front booth with her back to everyone, writing on a note pad as she ate her lunch. There were several people eating at different tables and booths, and she seemed to have isolated herself from all of them. She turned occasionally, and they glanced at each other.

Jim had a great Southern meal that included cabbage and rutabagas. He left a tip on the table, turned and spoke to Mr. and Mrs. Clark, who were now seated right behind him at a table. "Should I just leave the dishes on the table? "Yes," They agreed, "Just leave them on the table." "Are you the owners of the business here?" Jim asked. "Yes." He said. "We have been established here for a long time. We live in the Monroeville area. My wife and I have been married for fifty three years and we have run this bakery and restaurant most of the time." "I'll bet things have changed since you first started here in this business." "Yes they have and I don't think it is for the better. Everything seems so much more complicated and confusing. People's values have changed it seems. One thing, young people just can't sustain a marriage for any length of time like me and my wife. Families are fragmented and broken. Divorce rates have soared." "Yes, Jim said, Life seemed so much more meaningful and simpler in the old days." "Yes, He said, we didn't need nearly as many lawyers then as we do today." When he said lawyers, Jim thought of the lady sitting in the front booth. He had already realized that she was probably a young lawyer. Jim said, "Yes and things were probably a whole lot cheaper back then. By the way, I'm looking for road Forty-Seven that goes west out of town. Can you tell me how to get to it?" The lady asked Jim if he meant toward U.S. Highway Eighty-Four and he said yes, that was the way he wanted to go. They both laughed and said that the road out front was Forty-Seven. All he needed to do was drive on west on that road. Jim thanked them for being so helpful. As he left the restaurant he glanced at the lady sitting in the booth up front. She returned his favor and seemed to say, "Yes, I'm a lawyer and that's why I am sitting up here!" Jim believed the owners also thought he was a lawyer. He was dressed in his usual black and white. Jim traveled on west on Forty Seven toward the place he really meant to find that day.

Chapter Sixteen

J im knew that Betsy Lee still occupied a place in his heart, a place he couldn't let go. She had influenced his reluctance with Angela, though he had not seen her for over thirty years. They could have so easily been life partners, Jim believed, but he had hesitated at that crucial moment. He had let an opportunity of a lifetime pass by. Or so he thought at the time. A little while back, he had begun to look for a way to meet her again that would help bring some closure to his feelings of regret. He conducted a computer search and was surprised at what he found. She had lived in various places but had recently lived in Lakeshore on Shady Oaks Drive. Presently she lived in Lakeshore in a condominium on Dauphin Drive. She is the president of a business that deals in real estate. She and her husband are well off financially, multi-millionaires he had been told. She had not married again, after she left Roy, until nineteen hundred ninety-eight. Jim sent her a birthday card about a year ago, when he learned from James Taylor where she was, but never received any reply or any correspondence from her. He sent her another one last December. Jim wrote a note inside. He said he understood she was happily married and he was married with a family himself. Jim mentioned he would never forget those Volkswagen days of long ago and that he thought she knew why. He described Joseph and Samuel to her and the pride he had in them for their accomplishments. Jim said he would like to see her one more time before he left this old earth if she would permit. He never received any reply of any kind. Jim knew the place in Lakeshore where their business was located, so he decided to go there one day. He went late one afternoon and finally found their office building. By the office door was a placard: "Betsy Lee Taylor Hilton Realtor".

When he turned the door knob to the office, it was locked. He gently rattled the door to be sure it would not open. Jim started to turn and leave when the door opened. Betsy Lee had opened the door. He looked at her and she looked at him, and the chasm of thirty years or more was finally broken. It took her a moment, but then she exclaimed, "Mr. Josephson!" They almost embraced, but Betsy Lee glanced at another woman sitting in an adjoining room and Jim hesitated. "Come on in, Jim. Goodness, it's been a long time. It's good to see you. You came in just at the right time. My husband just left. I mean you must have passed him outside." "I didn't see anybody outside." Jim said. As Jim stepped forward she turned toward the lady that was sitting in the other room. "Jim, this is Mrs. Simpson, my secretary." To her, she said: "This is Jim Josephson, an old friend. He's the one that sent me the birthday card." "Hello." Jim said. "It's nice to meet you." "It's nice to meet you." She said. "Jim, come on over here and sit down at my desk where we can talk." "Ok." he said. When Jim sat down, He said. "I always knew you would be successful. And look! Now you are the president of a company! How have you been, Betsy Lee"? "Oh, I have been doing well. I stay busy here. You know, Jim, you chose just the right time to come here. If you had come any time sooner my husband would have been here. That wouldn't have been good. He's the jealous type and it's good he's not here. You timed that just right." "Well, I just walked up to your office. I thought it was closed. I didn't know. I didn't see anyone. So you got the birthday card. I sent you one before. Did you get that one?" "No. I never got that one. You sent me one on my birthday before this last one?" She asked. "Yes." Jim said. "I have sent you two of them." "Well, I have gotten only one, the one where you mentioned your children." "Yes." Jim said "That was the last one." "I wonder why I never got the first one." She said. "Where did you send it? Here, where you sent the last one?" "No." Jim said. "I sent it to your residence at the condominium." "Well, I wonder what happened." "How did you find out where I am?" She asked. "I went by James' house in Taylorville, and he told me you were in town. He said your mother had passed away. I found your mother's obituary and saw that you were living in Lakeshore. I thought you had gone to

California or somewhere. I didn't know you were here." "I did go to Washington State for a while. I wonder why James never told me of your visit." She said. "Oh, it wasn't that long ago." Jim said. "Gosh Betsy, you never married again until 1998! That was just a short time ago. I thought you had someone you were going to marry after you left Roy." "No—No—Well I went back to school and I stayed busy working." "What did you study, the real estate business?' Jim asked. "No. I studied medicine." "Medicine!" Jim exclaimed. "Yes, I studied Medicine." She said. "Betsy, do you remember the window just above the door of your old shop?" "Yes, I remember the window. It was a long, narrow window." "Every time I would ride by the old shop I would look up at that window, and I could see you standing there. You know I liked you a lot back then." She hesitated for a moment. "That was my problem. A lot of people liked me back then, but you were one of my favorites." I saw her glance around toward her secretary. "All we did was talk, but we talked a lot." She said. Jim knew she said this for the benefit of the other lady who was listening and it was true but he felt that uneasy feeling creep up again of missed opportunity because he knew it had been there and now she seemed to be saying that herself. "I know you must be a person of commitment?" Jim questioned. "Yes. I am. I'm a person of commitment." She confirmed. "Well I am, too, Betsy." Jim admitted. "I went to Roy's funeral the other day, Betsy." "What!" She exclaimed. "Roy died!?" She was shocked! "Yes." Jim said. "You didn't know?" He questioned. "No." "I didn't know anything about it. What in the world happened? What was wrong with him?" She asked. "I don't know what caused his death. I read about it in the newspaper. I went there looking for you. I thought you might be there. That wasn't the *only* reason of course, but I was hoping I would see you there. You know I liked Roy, Betsy." "Oh yeah, Roy was a likeable person. The thing I couldn't handle, though, was his lying. He would falsify records and lie about all kinds of things." "I just couldn't handle that." She said. "Do you own any part of the old business?" Jim asked. "No! I got out of there with my life!" She exclaimed. "I've written a book about all of that, Betsy." I said. "You mean about back then? You remember about all of that, everything?"

"Yes." Jim said. "I remember everything." "Oh my goodness!" She exclaimed. She turned toward her secretary. "Some people have said I should write a book!" "Do you ever go back to Taylorville where you lived as a child?" Jim asked. "Yes! I go back there and spend a day or two on the farm I own up there. I get away to the country where I relax and work with the plants and flowers. I haven't been back recently, though. My husband doesn't like for me to go there. He is so jealous of me. So I don't go often any more. We go to Europe, though. We go four months out of every year." "Wow, Betsy! You get to go to Europe every year! "Yes, we go to Germany and all over visiting my husband's people and the places he used to live." "But what about the country where you lived as a child Betsy? Do you like that, the country life and everything?" "Yes—Yes, I do." When she said she did, their eyes met again in that embrace of long ago. "It's like going home, isn't it?" "Yes—Yes. It's like going home." Jim knew she felt the emotion that flooded over him in that moment as tears began to form in his eyes. She knew it was what Jim wanted her to do back then. To go home, to go home to the place he thought she loved, for both of them to go home together. Jim had wanted so much for them to be one together. They had so much to offer each other. He thought at one time she had considered this. Once she told him that he might just be what she really needed. Remorsefully, he knew they would never know. Jim knew it was time for him to leave then. "Well, Betsy' I need to be going on. It's getting late, and I have a way to go. It was good to see you again." "Yes, I need to close up and go. My husband will be wondering where I am. It was so good to see you, too." Jim stood up and started toward the door. She accompanied him to the door. As he opened the door to go out, He turned and said "Maybe I will see you again one day." Jim saw her draw back ever so slightly and he knew it would likely not happen.

Jim came away with a burden lifted, with a new spark of relief and happiness to have seen her. She must realize now how much Jim loved her. He knew any chance of being together had passed with the thirty or more years that had unfolded. But he knew he still had a friend that cared, something he had been denied recently.

Chapter Seventeen

O
n down old Road Forty-Seven Jim went to U.S. Highway Eighty-Four and Taylor's Road where he thought he might find the farm that Betsy said she owned. Yes, the farm. Jim wanted to see the farm. He thought it might have been inherited from her mother, but he didn't know. Jim found Taylor's Road on Eighty-Four past a small convenience store. He stopped at the store to use the restroom and talk with the people who worked there. He asked them about Betsy Lee, and her family but no one knew anything about her or her former husband. Jim thumbed through the local phone book but did not find anything he didn't already know. He drove down the country clay road to a turn to the left. Off to the right on the turn was a vacant home with some property around and in the back of it. It was a fairly large home but not what Jim really expected to find. He passed on by after checking the mailbox for a name. There was no name. On down the road on the left was another home. Obviously, one not associated with a farm. Jim decided to stop and ask about her, if anyone should happen to be home. There were no cars or other vehicles parked there. He knocked on the door and a young woman with a child standing beside her answered the door. Jim said, "Good morning, Mam. I just stopped to ask you a question if you don't mind." She said, "Sure, go ahead. What would you like to know?" When she said this their eyes had met and there was a strong attraction drawing them like a magnet to one another. Her eyes were deep and emotional, filled with intelligence and compassion. They reminded him a little of Betsy Lee. "No! No! Jim" He said to himself, "You just came from Burnt Corn." How beautiful and how easy life could be, but that is not all there is to living. Jim thought to himself, "Is it a fault of mine that seems to

make this happen so often?" He interrupted their gaze with, "I just wanted to know if a person named Betsy Hilton had a farm around here somewhere. She said, "Betsy Hilton? I don't know anyone by that name." Jim said, "She was Betsy Taylor before she married." "Oh, I am a Taylor," she said, but I don't know anyone by that name." "I thought the farm might be around here somewhere on Taylor Road." Jim said, "I wondered about the vacant home on the corner with the property around it." She replied, "My husband lived there once but he moved to Lakeshore for a while before he came back here to this place, but I don't know about anyone named Betsy Taylor." She was holding a small dog, and Jim started a conversation about her dog. He spoke with the small girl that accompanied her. She was very relaxed and very receptive toward this stranger. Jim had made another friend even under the most difficult of circumstances. Jim thanked her for being so kind and helpful to a stranger. She said that was no problem, she was very glad to help. Jim thanked her again and walked back to his truck. The road was a loop, and he came back out on U.S. Highway Eighty-Four. He drove down to another loop road that was also named Taylor Road. He stopped a postal carrier and asked her about the farm, Betsy Lee Hilton and Betsy Lee Taylor. She said she could not divulge any information to anyone, this was against the law. And then she did what Jim had done with some of his students in school many times. She informed him, but she didn't inform him. Students would come to his desk looking for answers to questions on worksheets and he would tell them: "If I could tell you the answer to the question was "atom", I would, but I can't tell you what the answer is. You will need to find that out yourself." Some students would stop and look at him with a smile and turn away, back to their desks. Others would go off puzzled looking for the answer! This was just another way of grading the awareness of a student, and he enjoyed watching the students react. The postal carrier had indirectly informed him she did not know of anyone around this area who owned a farm named Betsy Hilton or Betsy Taylor. They laughed and talked for a moment, and became friends. She laughed and said, "You could be a terrorist!" They laughed again and Jim said, "I could be, but I'm not!" She knew Jim was not a terrorist. She even knew he was the kind of person she could trust, a humble man with character and caring. This is why Jim could make friends so easily and one reason his life was so complex.

Jim would need to use other resources to find the farm if he ever decided to do so. He knew he could always ask James, but that was too personal. He really didn't know what Betsy might think about his inquiries. She wouldn't care as far as she was concerned, but her relationship with her husband might make it a different matter. Jim took an old highway back into the town of Taylorville where she had lived for a time after her father had passed away. He drove down First Street as he had before, and James was there. His truck was in the drive in front of his fall garden of greens. His home was in front of an open court with a school on the other side. Jim wondered again for a moment. He had taught thirty-five years in a school such as this. He wondered what it might have been like to have had James for a brother in law. They share many of the same interests. James seems to be a very upright and considerate person. He was a deer hunter as Jim had been so long ago. Jim drove on out of Taylorville on his way back home. He stopped at a small café in Farmville, Alabama to get a cup of coffee and a bite to eat. He talked with the owner for a while, mostly about politics. She asked Jim a lot of questions about himself and his home. She also had connections to Lakeshore and the fast life on the beaches. She was interested in Jim, he knew. She always had been. Jim left Farmville and drove back toward his home on Court Street in Lakeshore. He went south west on Old Stagecoach Road 5 and turned left on Road Forty-Five below Goodway and down through some of the most beautiful farming country to State Road Twenty-Seven, the old Sardine Route. He went south east on Twenty-Seven, crossed the Big Escambia Creek to Stanley Crossroads. At Stanley Crossroads, He took Twenty-Five south down the east side of Big Escambia Creek to Flomaton on the Alabama Florida Line. He drove down Old Palafox Highway through Flomaton to Florida State Road Four. Jim crossed the Escambia River Bridge into Santa Rosa County and turned right on Morristown Road. He took the Chumukla Highway to County Highway One Seventy-Eight and

One Seventy-Eight to Highway Eighty-Nine. He traveled down Highway Eighty Nine to the old Ward's Store crossroads and turned left on Central School Road. Jim crossed the Allentown highway to A. D. McCall Road. At the dead end he turned left on Jessie Allen Road. Allentown was named after the family of Jessie Carter Allen who lived there when he was the first sheriff of Santa Rosa County, the county Jim was now in. He was Jim's second great grandfather on his grandmother Jernigan's, mother's, side of the family. Jessie Carter Allen's parents were the ones who died at Fort Mims. This is why Jim had taken this route, to pass by the old Allen home place. Jim's great grandfather Jernigan also lived on this road many years ago. He married Jessie Carter Allen's daughter, Margaret Hughana Allen. He was a descendant of high-ranking Indian ancestors of the Cherokee, Chickasaw, and Powhatan Nations from his father's, mother's side of the family. Jessie Allen Road leads to Highway Eighty-Seven the road Jim intersected on his way from Lakeshore. He traveled back west, the way he had come, and eventually intersected Highway Twenty-Nine to Lakeshore, turned right on Court Street and right again to his home where Dorothy, Joseph and Jim live.

As Jim traveled these roads home through beautiful country of hamlets, woodlands and farms and was moved by the scenery, the places and people, he thought about what this was all about and what he was all about. Dorothy knew he understood real love. Dorothy had experienced what he was capable of giving. Jim had given to her for over thirty years, what he had wanted to give to Betsy Lee at one time. He could not give this gift again. It was Dorothy's to have and to hold, to keep. One cannot turn back the hand of time. What Jim would not break was at the heart of what he had desired to give Betsy Lee in the first place; trust, caring, unwavering commitment, unbroken faithfulness and a family to love and cherish. Jim treasured these things. They were his life, his love, the essence of his being. "Have you ever been to Burnt Corn?" Jim reflected: "Yes, I have. I go there often and the air is fresh and clean, the sky is clear and blue and I rejoice in the love and happiness that is mine

Chapter Eighteen

As time passed on by and Jim began to readjust after all of the experiences he had encountered at Lakeview Baptist Church, He learned that his Nephew's Father-in-law, Mr Joel, had passed away. Jim had visited with Mr. Joel several times in the last year. He was suffering from upper respiratory disease and had been fairly inactive. He was eighty nine years old. He had been the Older Men's class treasurer while Jim was attending Lakeview Baptist Church. Jim had seen him a couple of times hunting with his nephew and the few remaining members of his father's old hunting party on Yellow River. Mr. Joel and Jim's nephew were very close and they were all part of the larger family. Jim planned to attend the visitation and funeral services. The services were to be held at Lakeview Baptist Church. The visitation was at night at six till nine o'clock in the church sanctuary. Dorothy could not attend the visitation that night because of a conflict so Jim attended alone. Jim knew he would be received well by the members of his family and his friends at Lakeview Baptist Church but he was apprehensive about T. W. Davis, his family and friends. They were leaders in the Church and community and their influence was widespread throughout the area. They would surely be there. They were friends with Mr. Joel and his family also. Jim knew they would respect his presence there because of the family but wasn't sure just how they would respond to him personally. Jim had noticed some negative vibes among the close friends of T. W. Davis especially the female ones. He knew that T. W. had tried to claim to some of his close friends that Jim had a personal problem about approaching women. He did this to protect his daughter's reputation among church members and friends. Jim knew that many members of Lakeview Baptist Church did not buy this slant that T. W. was giving this unfortunate happening at Lakeview. He had learned some members had questioned Angela's behavior even before anything had occurred between them. Jim resolved to meet them publicly at the visitation and force them to react to his presence around people who would notice.

Jim arrived at the church about an hour after the immediate family had been scheduled to meet. The church was almost filled with friends and relatives and a long line of visitors awaited their time to give condolences to the family and pay their respect to Mr. Joel. Jim was greeted warmly by his nephew and family. His nephew told Jim he knew he would be there. Indicating he knew nothing would stop Jim from coming to the visitation of a dear friend he loved. Jim was amazed at the people that warmly greeted him in the awaiting line and was uplifted with the opportunity to meet and talk to friends he hadn't seen for quite some time. Jim was able to converse with several of the members of the Older Men's Class. After meeting with the family at the bier and giving his last farewell to a dear friend he looked down the receding isle and noticed T. W. and his two sons talking with some of their friends who were gathered around. Jim moved slowly on down through the people standing there greeting and speaking with some of them until he reached T. W. and his sons. As he approached them they formed a closed circle and turned their backs to him. It was obvious to the visitors close by; some he had just greeted. Jim did not turn away but kept pressing until an opening occurred so he could step forward and greet them face to face. Jim extended his hand to T. W. "Hello T. W. It is good to see you." He reluctantly shook Jim's hand but didn't respond. Jim turned to his sons. "I just wanted to stop and say hello and to let you know that I love you and all of your family." This comment while others stood watching and listening broke the ice and they responded to Jim warmly. Jim moved on down the aisle toward the door meeting and greeting other friends and relatives. Jim knew Mr. Joel would be proud of him for greeting them with Christian love and not harboring hatred in his heart regardless of how he had been treated. It was easy for Jim to do this. Mr. Joel loved T. W. and his family and so did Jim.

Chapter Nineteen

The funeral had reawakened some of the emotional experiences Jim had encountered in his life, especially those surrounding Angela and Betsy lee. Angela had been a dear but unwanted, unfortunate happening that had been very hard for Jim to rationally understand and reconcile with his deep values of church and family. His belief that some of his questionable activities of long ago may have been part of the precipitating element did not make it any easier. The implementation of this experience had not been Jim's doing and had not been his desire. It had happened nevertheless. Betsy Lee was a different matter. Betsy Lee was and always had been a special person to Jim from the first time he had seen her. The feelings and attraction between them had been mutual and he had perused her favor and love. He had fallen in love with her, whatever that could mean under the circumstances, because true love to Jim meant a righteous relationship and ultimate commitment. This had happened, of course, before he ever dated Dorothy. One nagging regret remained unaddressed and just would not pass on by no matter how much he was committed to Dorothy or how much he loved her and their family. He realized he had to see Betsy Lee one more time. He had to do it. For over thirty-five years it had been an unresolved heartache. It was not the unfulfilled physical desire although that was always an influence. That had faded long ago. It was like the love of his lost mother and lost father, lost aunt and lost uncle and the joy that had been his because of it. It was like an old southern son trying to verbalize to his dying father that he loved him. Jim could not let his life pass on by without speaking, without speaking his heart.

Jim had agreed to go by the Sears warehouse and pick up a new dish washer for Dorothy's mother. It was very close to Betsy Lee's business office, so he decided to go by on the way home. Jim drove through the Lakeview Mall and by the movie theater in the rear and stopped in front of the complex of office buildings behind it. He walked behind a row of cars parked on the curb and glanced at the tag numbers as he passed by, wondering which one could be Betsy Lee's. Jim became a little apprehensive as he approached the door to her office. It was about ten o'clock in the A.M, and the area seemed unusually quiet. Jim wondered if Betsy was there. He glanced again at the plaque by the office door, "Betsy Lee Taylor Hilton Realtor". A feeling of admiration swept through him. Jim always knew she would be successful and just to see her name there rekindled some of the deep emotions and feelings Jim had always had for her. He rang the door bell and waited. He didn't know if her husband was there. The door opened, and there was Betsy Lee again. She seemed startled to see him and stepped forward, obviously blocking him from the office inside. "I just dropped by to say hello." Jim said. "Oh Jim, I—I'm not sure you should be here. Let's walk around the front of the buildings where we can talk. I need to take a look at something around there." "Ok." Jim said. "I just stopped by to say hello. I had to come over and pick up a washing machine for my mother-in-law at Sears, so I came by here." As they walked along the sidewalk, they began to talk and it was obvious to Jim she was trying to make this look like a business meeting between herself and an officer or adjuster. They approached a car parked on the curb. "You see this car? This goes on all the time. People just don't seem to care anymore. It's been here for days." "Look, it has a dented fender." Jim said. She jotted some notes on a note pad she had. She turned to Jim, "Do you remember, Jim, when you came by here one Sunday, and my secretary was here with some workers cleaning up the buildings and grounds? The next day in the office, she said to me in front of everyone that was there, "Your boyfriend came by to see you yesterday." If my husband had heard that, you don't know what kind of trouble I would have been in. You just can't imagine what

I have been going through lately, my husband is so jealous." "I wouldn't mind meeting your husband if that would"—"No, no.", she interrupted, "I wouldn't want that to happen." She said. "He wouldn't be nice to you, and I just wouldn't want that to happen to you. He would be ugly toward you, and I don't want that. It has gotten really bad for me here lately. I can't do anything. He is so jealous. I can't even be with my family like I should." "You know, I wondered about that," Jim said. "What did he do? Lock you up in a maximum security condominium so you couldn't get out?" "Yeah—that's what it is it seems. I just don't know what—you know, I have had two husbands and I have made both of them rich." Jim looked at her when she said this, and Betsy knew what Jim was thinking. They could have been a team together and then both of them would have had everything, not just the riches, everything. "You made them rich?" Jim questioned. "Yes, I made them rich. I just know how to get things done. Greg,(her husband) he doesn't know. He is one of those people who would get confused trying to use a screwdriver." "You made yourself rich." Jim said. She shrugged at this as if something was yet missing. "Do you own all of these buildings here?" Jim asked. "My husband does." She said. "You know, you said last time that you had a farm in the country." "Oh, yes. But that farm—it's mostly just swamp—Jim, have you ever gotten to the point where you didn't know if you could take it any longer?" Jim stepped toward her as she filled with tears and emotion and reached out to embrace her but the openness, and knowledge of her apprehension stopped him short. "I am so sorry Betsy Lee, I am so sorry, you know—I mean—that you are having this difficulty. Listen, I won't come back any more. I won't come back. I didn't know what kind of relationship we could have, but not even a casual one?" "No" She said. "No—Not even a casual one." Jim realized then that he was causing her marriage to be in jeopardy, or her other intentions if she had been planning any. "If he feels this way, if he is so jealous of you—you know he must really care for you." Jim said. Betsy Lee stood silent and looked off into her world for the briefest moment, and Jim knew her deepest feelings were not with him. "Betsy Lee, I will always care for you.

I will never stop caring for you. You were so gracious and kind, so intelligent and so beautiful. I wouldn't be here talking after thirty years if I didn't care, would I?" "No." She said. She turned toward Jim and their eyes met again, "You know I care don't you?" "I will always care." "Yes." She said—"I know you care." "I had to come here, Betsy Lee, I had to come. I had to come and get this off my shoulders." "Why could I not just say, "I love you, Betsy Lee?" Jim thought. She knew this was what he was saying. She knew this from the very beginning years ago." Jim wanted to say he would give up everything, but he knew he couldn't. It was the essence of the very love Jim had for Dorothy *and* her, and the promises he had made to Dorothy for her love that stopped him. In his own mind and for his own spiritual need, Jim knew that a wrong could not make a right, right. It would destroy the very thing that made it right. And Jim knew, because of this, the right would always remain right, clear and clean and beautiful. Betsy's mood brightened and she commented with excitement, flashing that beautiful smile, "I am going to Europe." "You are going to Europe?" Jim questioned. You said you went there every summer the last time I was here. When are you going?" "Next Monday. We leave on the plane for Europe this next Monday." She stepped toward Jim, extended her hand and he took it in his. "I am sorry, Jim, so sorry—I am so sorry." "Don't be sorry," Jim said. "I won't come back. I won't come back." She turned from Jim and started back to the office. He watched her leave for a moment and walked back to his truck. He wanted so much to offer her what he had always wanted to give. Jim knew she would have loved him and he knew they would have been financially successful. But together they would have been so much more for each other. Jim wanted her to be the mother of his family and bear his children. He couldn't offer that gift now, the years had removed that possibility. Jim had given this to Dorothy. Betsy Lee knew this just as she knew she was committed to her marriage for whatever reasons of her own.

What would life have been had he kissed her that day? But the spirit of love and goodness that people can share cannot be destroyed by the whims and chance of an unfolding world. Jim will always care for her in the deepest reaches of his heart. Betsy Lee knows that now.—Well, Jim learned to fly airplanes, J3's and others. Jim never flew an F16 but he knew he could have.

Jim traveled back across the bay on the interstate bridge, and as he passed over the arch of the channel, he looked out over the bay and the beautiful scenery there. He looked down the bay toward the condominium where she lived. Jim was filled with emotion hard to describe; great joy to have known her and to know she had cared, great admiration for her accomplishments, great remorse for expectations and needs not realized, great wonder at what might have been. Jim went through Lakeshore on Highway Ninety-Eight and drove passed Roy's old Volkswagen shop. He looked for the window that was no longer there. His mind flashed back, and he saw her standing there, vibrant and beautiful, laughing and smiling. Visions of what could have been, what might have been, kept flowing through his mind.

It was late when Jim finally turned toward Court Street and the home he had built for Dorothy and the boys. Jim came in through the garage door and Dorothy was there working on her computer as usual. "Did you get the washing machine for mother?" She called out from the computer room. "Yes, I picked it up. It is on the back of the truck. I will carry it over there tomorrow some time." "Ok." She said. Jim took off his light jacket, hung it on the back of his chair and sat down at his desk. He felt a little uneasy with all of the reminiscing about dreams of long ago. Dreams that he knew had long since passed over the waterfall of life to be lost in the churning currents of reality. Dorothy had given him more than any other woman in his life and Dorothy was heavy on his heart as he sat there. He felt strongly he needed to reassure Dorothy's love and trust for him. He felt he needed to reinforce his commitment and feelings for her because he knew now, deep down, that his pledge and commitment to her and their family were the most important things in his life, promises he could not break. To break his promises with Dorothy would also break a covenant with himself, that inner self that powers his hopes and aspirations. He picked up a piece of stationary and began to write.

To Dorothy

What does it mean to a man for a woman to be loyal and faithful, to understand the big things and disregard the little things? It is like the aircraft engine that you bet your life on and the landing gear that takes your slight drift on the runway. It is like the Sage that knows the depths of your real heart, but understands your human condition. Amid my consternation over lost dreams and unattainable yearnings I have always heard the quiet reassuring whisper, "I love you Jim". No other woman has ever said that to me so many times and meant it every time. I was always the dreamer. The great adventure was just over that next hill or beyond that sinking sunset. I have been sometimes like the man who was looking for a higher place to stand so as to gain a better and grander view, and after looking all around, realized he was standing on the highest possible ground and had the best possible view. No, not yearning to quit or to break promises but just yearning, yearning for a passed moment or an unrealized dream. Just yearning like every man does, only with powerful feeling and emotion. I have learned lately that the real dream is already in my hand and the others are vapors that evaporate with the burning rays of reality and the constancy of daily devotion and commitment. We have never sung a duet together but we have sung a song of life together, a greater song, a profound and powerful song, a song of family, of day by day caring and commitment, a day by day love song that is always there and is the real fulfillment of my most sought after dreams. Now I would like to draw you close and whisper in your ear, for now and forever "I love you Dorothy."

He carefully folded the letter and put it in an envelope. He wrote "To Dorothy" on the outside. He walked over to Dorothy's chair and picked up her Bible that lay on the table next to it. He turned to Chapter Thirteen of the first book to the Corinthians and placed the letter between the pages and returned it to the table. Jim sat down in the old chair his Grandmother Carter had purchased so long, long ago that sits in his family room. It was the one his dad sat in after a hard day's work and a great supper prepared by his loving wife, Jim's mother. He would sit in it until he went to sleep and Jim would watch him there, snoring in a peaceful sleep because home was his heaven. Jim loved this man so much. He knew much of it was because his mother loved him so much. She always upheld him. She made him and his children the purpose for her life. Jim loved her deeply and she loved him, almost to a fault. Jim remembered when his first wife left him. He would sit in that chair in the living room of their old home and find peace when he couldn't find it anywhere else. And now, Jim sat there, and those memories began to sustain him. Jim glanced at the chair his Uncle Oliver sat in when he would come to talk deer hunting with his dad. A peace came over him, and he slipped off to sleep in the old chair, and began to dream—

Jim had grown much older now. He must have been in his nineties. He was still in good health and alert mentally. He decided to go over to Bill Colson's private field and see if he would let him solo his old J-3 Cub again. Bill had purchased his old plane and kept it in his hanger at the field. With some reluctance, he agreed to check him out to see if he could possibly do this. Well, Jim surprised him. His old touch came back from all those years of flying this plane, and he could fly it as good if not better than Bill. Bill decided to let him take it out solo. Jim left his field at Harold, Florida and headed out West North West toward the old farm fields north of Allentown just west of the Whiting Field controlled air space. He began to do aerobatics over the fields as he had done years ago. He did loops, hammerhead turns, chandelles, Immlemans, and steep turns. He was having a ball. Then he decided to do one of his favorite maneuvers, the vertical spin. It was a joy to do in an old J-3. Jim climbed to about three thousand feet and started to execute the maneuver. He pulled the power back to idle and maintained altitude by increasing the back pressure on the old joy stick. When the airspeed indicator had passed by the twenty mark, the old door flopped up, the J-3's own unique stall indicator. As the door flopped up, the plane started to drop. He kept the old joy stick crammed back into his belly and quickly popped the left rudder pedal to the floor and held it there. The old J-3 quickly rolled left, pitched nose down and began to spin around its vertical axis. Jim could see the fields he loved spinning below him, and he just let it spin and tighten up a bit. He saw the upper wing when it separated from the fuselage and flew back over the tail section. The plane pitched more violently down and accelerated greatly toward the ground. He could see the cotton field turning wildly below him getting ever larger and larger. In the instant he saw the blur of the cotton on the stalks, He awakened from his dream—And found himself—Sitting in the Volkswagen in front of his old home—kissing Betsy Lee—And then he slipped off into another dream—

He dreamed he was standing by the Holy Wall on the Holy Hill in Jerusalem. Crowds of all kinds of people were all around. He could see Jews with their yarmulkes, Christians with their bibles, Moslems with their kuffiyehs. There were others there, people from countries all over the world who had come to view this Holy killing place called Palestine. Yes, even Jerusalem, the Holy Killing place of not only the body but the soul in a Holy Land of war. Yes, Jerusalem, a living oxymoron. His heart was poured out; his vision broken like pot shards lying on the Holy Hill. His inner being began to cry with a loud voice in the languages of the peoples that had gathered there. It reverberated off the wall of tears and hope, echoed through the Dome of the Rock, and flowed out across the Holy Hill of Calvary as if a Holy Wind had taken it there. He began to preach with the deepest essence of his being. He saw his Holy places flood through his mind, the Belandville road, the woodlands, the farmlands, the hamlets, towns and cities, where he had searched for the Holy God in his soul, where he had become a man of sorrow acquainted with grief. He cried out with a loud voice:

Stop! Stop now and harken unto the voice of righteousness,
The voice, cleansed with the fire of righteousness,
Calling from the mountains and hills
Embellished by Holy Shrines,
Weeping in sackcloth and ashes,
And remembering in utter despair.
Hear His Holy Word moving,
Speaking in profound regret,
"What a disgusting sight to all mankind!
*I see the cold dead bodies of rebellion against only Him."*3

Oh slayer of the Jew,
Oh slayer of the Arab,
Oh slayer of the Christian,
Oh slayer of mankind!
When will you stop your slaying?
Oh Jerusalem! Jerusalem!
Jerusalem in tears by your hand!

For what does our Lord God call,
And for what does our Lord God demand,
That we should be called His people?
A spear through the heart of offenders?
A sword as the keeper of his will?
His disgust is the blade of the sword!
His rejection has called the marching armies!

Cry out the reverent praises!
Oh hear! Oh hear! The Lord our God is one God!
Make clear the profound proclamations!

---

3   Isaiah 66:24, (MKJV), A personal 21st Century Reflection

God is only one! God is Great! God is Great!
Long live God!
Speak forth the moving testimonies!
Jesus is Lord! Jesus is Lord! Jesus saves!
But what does the Spirit of God within us
desire from the hand of his people?
For what does it beg?

I hear the longing cry of our Servant,
Prophet, Savior!
We see his pleading will for all mankind.
None are left without his promise!
He stands weeping at the sepulcher
Of His Holy Fathers!
Oh Jerusalem! Jerusalem!
House of Jehovah, of Ala and of God!
Stumbling still
At the truth of His Righteous Will!
Oh let the light shine
And clear our clouded minds
For the praise of our Holy One!

It is love not doctrine!
It is love more than martyrdom!
It is justice for the poor more than ceremony!
It is kindness rather than rebellion!
It is brotherhood rather than hatred!
It is to join hands not swords!
It is giving more than taking!
It is others more than self!
It is tolerance more than custom!
It is to relinquish and thus to save!
His hope is for your hearts!
This is his Jerusalem!
When will we ever learn?
Rebuild the broken walls

Within our hearts
For all mankind!

Hear! Hear! All who long for justice!
Hear the word of him who touches souls
With the majesty of his Spirit!
What would He have you teach
Your precious children,
The ones we cry for,
With deep and moving lamentation?
Hatred for all men,
In a false claim to glory?
Hatred for the children of our father
Abraham?
Territoriality and selfish pride?

The child becomes the mirror of our own
hatred.
We paint the pictures of his soul!
Look! Look deeply through that mirror,
oh men!
Humble your hearts and turn to your God!
Worship Him in spirit and in truth!
And then you will find you cannot teach
Your child to hate,
Even a Jew,
Even an Arab,
Even a Christian,
For God is Love in us all.
Oh precious day!
Oh Come with haste!
Oh precious day!

Jim heard the words "Blasphemer!", "Hypocrite!", "Heretic!", "Infidel!" as some in the crowd charged toward him. He felt the stones beginning to pelt his body. He cried out louder and louder, "It is love not doctrine!" "It is love not doctrine!" "Love is real!" "God is Love!" *"God is Love!"*, as a large stone hit him squarely in his temple. He stumbled forward bleeding and broken. His mind faded into a glorious sunrise filled with mist—And found himself—standing before the altar of his church—embracing the family of his spiritual soul.—And he heard the angles of heaven sing—Holy! Holy! Holy— "Holy is the Lord, Holy is the Lord!"—"Blessed are the flowers of spring."—And Jim awakened from his dream—

Dorothy was sitting on the couch next to the chair Jim was sleeping in, sewing on a quilt. She said to him as she had said so many times before in their life together—"You know I love you, Jim. You are the only one in all of my life for me. Why don't you go on to bed where you won't be so uncomfortable and can sleep in peace?" "Yes, Jim said. I've been sleeping here dreaming. "I love you too Dorothy, and our family, Joseph, Samuel, Aaron and Jill, our family Dorothy, our family of Josephsons." "Yes Jim, she said, our family, our family of Josephsons" as he retired to his room.

Postscript

This story in the life of the character Jim Josephson is authentic as told from the perspective of Jim Josephson. The letters and creative writings are documented and on file with other documents related to this story. The names have been changed and some places have been renamed to avoid any embarrassment or controversy. The last seven pages are derived from experiences of Jim Josephson in real life and in visions and dreams but are embellished in a creative presentation. There are many other events and happenings in the life of Jim Josephson that go untold in this story. They will be told, hopefully, by the people who knew and loved him.

The Author